William Ellery Channing

Harvard University Press

Cambridge, Massachusetts
and London, England
1981

William Ellery Channing

An Essay
on the
Liberal Spirit
in America

Andrew Delbanco

Publication of this book has been aided by a grant from the
Andrew W. Mellon Foundation
Library of Congress Cataloging in Publication Data

Delbanco, Andrew, 1952-
  William Ellery Channing : an essay on the liberal
spirit in America.

  Includes bibliographical references and index.
  1. Channing, William Ellery, 1780-1842.
BX9869.C4D44   288'.092'4 [B]   80-19304
ISBN 0-674-95335-5

to the memory of my mother

to my father

and to Dawn

Contents

Preface

WILLIAM ELLERY CHANNING has slipped away from us. We know him as an offstage presence, a reference point to which American writers frequently turn, but we have lost sight of him. Bryant, Parker, Henry Adams celebrated him. Emerson called him "our bishop." Whittier flatly, and accurately, declared that he had the greatest reputation in literature and religion of his time. Among the questions this book raises is what has happened to Channing, and why.

In a great essay published in 1951, Lionel Trilling asked and answered a similar question about William Dean Howells. "Somewhere in our mental constitution," Trilling wrote, "is the demand for life as pure spirit . . . We all piously know that man fulfills himself in society, yet we do not willingly consent to live in a particular society of the present." We have a "dislike of the conditioned," and "the extreme has become the commonplace of our day." Thus "we are not in a position to make a proper judgment of Howells, a man of moderate sentiments." This book is concerned with something like the same estrangement, for Channing too was a man of moderate sentiments. It was Emerson, not Channing, who wrote that "an institution is the lengthened shadow of one man . . . the Reformation, of Luther; Quakerism, of Fox; Methodism, of Wesley," and that he, Emerson, would live in the flesh, not the shadow. We have thrilled to Emerson's promise and example, and it has been harder to applaud Channing's more measured response to the problem of individuals and institutions. Finally, for Channing, an institution was the embodiment of hope for many men, a way to steer between the impulses of individuals, to provide an object of engagement other than the self. And yet Channing in his failing years stood up against slavery and the New England commerce it sustained—institutions toward which Emerson showed greater patience.

Channing lived a life of unresolved uncertainty. Though he hungered for something beyond the desiccated New England orthodoxy, he nevertheless consciously refused to take the step into transcendental enthusiasm that Emerson was to take. Restless within his inherited intellectual forms, Channing feared the potential demonism of the antinomian response. One great modern expression of that confirmed fear, Thomas Mann's *Doctor Faustus*, provides a telling echo of Channing's alarm: "I see in the church," says Leverkühn, "even as she is today, secularized and reduced to the bourgeois, a citadel of order, an institution for objective disciplining, canalizing, banking-up of the religious life, which without her would fall victim to subjectivist demoralization, to a chaos of divine and daemonic powers, to a world of fantastic uncanniness, an ocean of daemony." Emerson left his church. Channing, though outraged and saddened in his last years by his own congregation, did not.

He was born in April 1780 into a Newport family whose men were traditionally lawyers. He passed a cloistered childhood in the Rhode Island seaport, a town that Fenimore Cooper described in this way: "By a singular combination of circumstances . . . the merchants of Newport were becoming, at the same time, both slave dealers and gentlemen." Channing's family was not unimplicated in those circumstances.

After four years at Harvard and a regimen of reading in the Redwood Library, Channing entered the ministry at Boston and began to preach what Emerson called "sublime sermons every Sunday morning." The first decade at Federal Street was tranquil. The young minister softened on the issues of original sin and Christ's divinity, and pleased his sedate congregation not only with liberal doctrine but also by condemning the War of 1812—though he never preached secession. In 1815, settled and grown locally famous for his eloquence, he came to the defense of the beleaguered liberal clergy, who were being attacked in a series of polemical pamphlets. Through his contributions to that controversy Channing became permanently identified as the leading spokesman for the Unitarian cause, though he always denied the existence of such a party.

As a consequence of his newfound status, Channing was invited in 1819 to deliver the ordination sermon at the installation of Jared Sparks in the first Unitarian church in Baltimore. He preached a sermon on that occasion that became a classic of rational religion in America. It is a measure of the persistent centrality of religion in the early national period that Channing's Baltimore sermon circulated as widely as any American controversial tract until Webster's reply to Hayne in 1830. For the liberals it was a nearly sacred text; for the orthodox, an utterance of perfidy.

By the 1820s Channing had a national reputation, greatly augmented by a series of major publications: a study of Milton in 1826, an essay on Napoleon in 1828, the famous call for a national literature in 1830, and a great sermon published as "Likeness to God" in 1828 which anticipated much of the transcendentalist spirit. Europe took notice too. Channing was the object of punctual homage from Charles Dickens on his first American journey; for Sismondi he was a frequent correspondent; later, for Renan, the foremost example of American integrity. By his fiftieth year Channing was established as a New World sage, perhaps the first American since Franklin who could be legitimately counted, as one contemporary put it, among "those few men who can command the attention of the civilized world."

He had married his cousin Ruth Gibbs; they had four chil-

dren and owned a dignified house on Mt. Vernon Street. But it
was just at the moment of achieved stability and prestige that he
began to grow restive. His endorsement was now a coveted com-
modity. Soon the abolitionists came to solicit his support. Partly
under their pressure, but more from a pressure within, Channing
ceased in the 1830s to be the darling of the New England gentry
and became instead their most threatening critic. He stunned his
constituents with one antislavery tract after another, each moving closer to espousing outright abolition. Near the end of his life
he preached, against the explicit wishes of the Federal Street
Church committee, a funeral sermon for the abolitionist Charles
Follen—a minor but genuine classic of American prose. John
Greenleaf Whittier gave this account of Channing's repudiation
by his former constituency: "As to the matter of courage and
self-sacrifice, very few of us have evinced so much of both . . .
he threw upon the altar the proudest reputation, in letters and
theology, of his day." In rising against slavery Channing gave to
the cause of emancipation in America a new respectability, a
new defense against ridicule, and ultimately a stronger future.

He died in 1842. The chorus of tribute was large. He had
lived primarily a life of the mind, and it was finally at the insti-
gation, not the expense, of his intellect that he moved toward a
life of political action.

"The true object of biography," Channing said, "is to give us
an insight into men's characters, such as an intimate acquaintance with them would have furnished." In interpreting Channing's life, I have written with respect not only for his statement
but also for his mode of statement. His language, his ways of
expression, are my conduits into his mind. The premise of this
procedure is the conviction that a man's inner life may be
grasped through his public utterance. Biography, I believe,
should not make rigid separation between the external and the
internal—it is a false distinction because life belies it. But in a

work of this length one must inevitably rule out more than one rules in, and I have chosen to abbreviate outward detail, knowing that it is copiously recorded elsewhere, and hoping that of the two it is the more tolerable sacrifice. In treating the first two decades of Channing's life—the years before he became a public man—the narrative rests on private materials, letters, diaries, and the like. Upon ascending his pulpit Channing began the process of choosing what to say to the world and what to withhold from it. I have largely honored his choice. When I do examine private correspondence, it is mainly to test what I have inferred from the public record. I am not saying that one should believe only what a man publishes but rather that what a man publishes may reveal the private as well as the public self. Finally, I have concentrated on the published work because my hope is to help restore Channing to the canon of American literature; it is his books, not his letters, that justify that hope.

There is in Channing's life a certain paradoxical symmetry. As he grew older and philosophically more conservative, he adopted more liberal political positions. Theodore Parker, upon hearing of his death, put it this way: "His faculties grew brighter as age came upon him." Channing may have been a representative man, but he was not a common one. He exactly reversed the Emersonian dictum that "We are reformers in spring and summer, in autumn and winter we stand by the old." In 1841, on the eve of Channing's death, Emerson wrote in *Self-Reliance*: "If an angry bigot assumes this bountiful cause of Abolition, and comes to me with his last news from Barbadoes, why should I not say to him, 'Go love thy infant; love thy wood-chopper; be good-natured and modest; have that grace; and never varnish your hard, uncharitable ambition with this incredible tenderness for black folk a thousand miles off. Thy love affair is spite at home.' " Emerson was thirty-eight in the year he wrote those words, Channing sixty-one. This was, of course, not Emerson's final statement on abolition, but *Self-Reliance* does contain a serene condescension that he never entirely relinquished. One year before, Channing had stood before a half-comprehending congregation and delivered a funeral sermon in which he asked the dead Charles Follen to forgive him for his tardy enlistment in the cause.

Channing's religious, literary, and philosophical thinking all combined to draw him into political engagement, and so we must attempt to comprehend the unity of his thought rather than divide and distribute it into compartments. In our time Lionel Trilling has preeminently expressed and met this kind of critical responsibility, and I venture to apply his words once more to my effort: "The word liberal is a word primarily of political import, but its political meaning defines itself by the quality of life it envisages, by the sentiments it desires to affirm. This will begin to explain why a writer of literary criticism involves himself with political considerations. These are not political essays, they are essays in literary criticism. But they assume the inevitable intimate, if not always obvious connection between literature and politics."

Channing sensed the imminence of an abduction of creative passion by romantic individualism. He perceived that the cult of subjectivity and the urge toward reunion between nature and man must give way to something born between them. He feared the creature whose birth he expected. Unlike Leverkühn, he did not surrender himself to his prophecy, and as a consequence, he did not achieve the fire of great art. Some have called his choice cowardice, or impotence; I shall call it intelligence. My narrative is of a man divided against himself by the dual pull of reason and mystery. Living into the 1840s, Channing, though suited temperamentally to tradition, could no longer appeal to the past. That he could not reflects his moral honesty, because the great issues of his time testified against history. Christianity became for him fundamentally antihistorical, and the spokesmen for slavery denied him recourse to history by turning it to their own defense. While Emerson and his generation escaped from this limbo into transcendental joy, Channing stood still. His immobility has been called paralysis, and to some extent it was—but I believe that it was also a considered refusal, one that may even illuminate the progress in savagery that our century has made over his.

Acknowledgments

ONE PROBLEM with which I am concerned in this book is the old challenge of speaking personally through conventional form. Acknowledgment is a literary convention; I can only hope that those I thank here will recognize something beyond the dutiful. I must say first that my involvement with the themes of this book doubtless reflects my origins—from Jewish parents who fled Hitler, and who tried in their transplanted lives to retain that balance between hope and reason which is called liberalism. Whatever is worthwhile here derives ultimately from them. Many good friends also shaped my thinking during my study of Channing. Among them, Eric Himmel, who for years has tried to keep me honest, and John Klause read the entire manuscript and aided my revisions. My brother Nicholas saved me from some clumsy constructions and jangling phrases. Among my teachers I want especially to thank Herschel Baker, who has been an unfailing guide for me in recent years, and Warner Berthoff, in whose seminar I first encountered Channing, and who kindly read the manuscript as well. Walter Jackson Bate, to whom any fledgling biographer owes a general debt, followed and criticized my work through several drafts—for which I am fortunate and grateful. Daniel Aaron gave generously of his time and editorial skill, helping me to repair and improve the text. The Danforth Foundation proved that an institution can be warm and human; their support is gratefully acknowledged, as is that of the Mrs. Giles Whiting Foundation. The National Society of Arts and Letters lifted my spirits by honoring the manuscript with an award while it was still in its early stages. Marte Shaw of the Houghton Library and her counterparts at several other libraries within and outside Harvard eased my work by their helpfulness and good humor. Not only a marvelous typist, Judith Brudnick has been editor, critic, and friend. Finally, I must acknowledge my greatest debt apart from those attested in the dedication. In his great learning, his wisdom, and above all his integrity, Alan Heimert has shown me the highest possibilities of my profession. I have no illusion that this small book constitutes repayment to such a teacher, but I have tried to make it the best I can do.

William Ellery Channing

Prologue:
Family,
Childhood,
Youth

Dr. Channing, whilst he lived, was the star of the American
Church, and we then thought, if we do not still think, that he
left no successor in the pulpit. He could never be reported,
for his eye and voice could not be printed, and his discourses
lose their best in losing them.

—Ralph Waldo Emerson

NEWPORT IN the 1770s rose and fell in population with the
turns of fortune. Numbering nine thousand in 1774, the town
was thinned by war and yet boasted bigger mailbags than New
York, a city that could still be identified as "New York, near
Newport."[1] It was never more than the traffic of its wharves, but
rum barrels yielded cash and cash yielded stature; good families
mingled not only with bad but with those which were not families at all. It was a town of sailors and whores, blue bloods, Jews,
Moravians, Quakers, Episcopalians, Congregationalists, but
mostly a mass in transit from rank to rank. The aroma of rum to
some was the stench of slave trade to others. Into this Newport,
in April 1780, William Ellery Channing was born.

Hot in summer, damp the whole year round, the town inspired few rhapsodies from her nineteenth-century chroniclers;
of the Channings, only William Henry (who never lived there)

sings the ocean beauties—a fit reminder of the romantic bias
with which he assembled the memoir of his uncle. Indeed a certain grimness prevails in most other Newport recollections.
George Gibbs Channing, younger brother of the famous Channing, assigns his earliest memory to an island off the coast where
smallpox vaccinations were administered, sores and skin erup-
tions healed, and the patients' silver coins were purified in fire.
He recalls the heat and the stinging fumes of tar as the town
ropeworks burned on an August day: "The houses on the hill
were largely impregnated with [the smoke]."[2] The Channing
house, large, ungainly, absorbed its share of the soot and still
stands on that hill, on the corner of Spring and Mary streets,
adjacent to the Congregational meeting house to which the
family belonged. Both are within sight of the stately Trinity
steeple, where Newport's Anglicans worshipped in style.

But George's *Recollections* stress cold more than heat, and
the splendor of Trinity was a forbidden if tantalizing haven from
the meeting house, which "was cold as the north pole in winter."
"How could the minister [William Patten], by no means a warm-
blooded man, be expected to inflame the souls of his hearers. . .?
In the coldest weather, he was muffled to the chin. The softer sex
had foot stoves; but the live coals in these, when kindled at
home, were nearly *dead* before being placed at the head of the
pew."[3] When Emerson would later speak of "corpse-cold Unitarianism" he would exempt Dr. Channing, and the exception
was earned; the Channings had felt the same deprivation. Indeed, there is an almost pathetic yearning in the family memoirs
for a vital minister; they shook their heads at the halting periods
of Samuel Hopkins while grudgingly attending his sermons during Ezra Stiles's absence. Returning to their own church, they
submitted to Patten, who stoked no fires, and they dutifully dis-
approved of the one man in town who everyone agreed could
spark an audience: the elegant Anglican Theodore Dehon, who
preached in Trinity accompanied by an organ given by a famous

Newport visitor, Bishop Berkeley. Secretly, the Channings admired him.

The tall and dapper Dehon seemed to monopolize clerical charm in Newport, though George, who carried on a kind of window-shopping among the city churches, does confess that even the raw Baptists intrigued him. William, to be sure, is less frivolous than his brother in recounting early church experiences, but still the emotional roots of the latitudinarianism and antisectarianism that would characterize his Unitarian movement may be seen in this mobility of Newport churchgoing—a mobility inspired not by broad-mindedness but by discontent. The town had not forgotten how George Whitefield had captivated fifteen hundred people in Hopkins's church, with hundreds more pressing to the windows from outside.[4] An almost elegiac theme, the sorry state of preaching would grow into an intellectual concern for Channing's generation. What is notable here is the early identification of "puritan" severity—an indigenous American affliction—as the dull counterpart to Anglican energy. Even Whitefield was English.

"Newport life," said George Gibbs Channing, summing up, "was prosy enough." Indeed all the Channings, looking back, felt variously constrained to apologize for home, not so much for its fallen morals as for its excellence as a seedbed of hypocrisy. The problem with Newport was not so much licentiousness or gross impiety but rather a sinister combination of worldly obsessions with regular, even rote church-observance. Self-deception flourished; even the schoolteachers, with their air of constant suspicion, served "to inaugurate a systematic duplicity" in their students. George repeatedly reminds his readers—and himself—that Newport was not always a summer "watering-place," or an American "Baden-Baden," but that the town once had had a deeper authenticity, a life and meaning of its own, not a prostituted dependence on summer "fashionables."[5] His brother Edward (the future mentor of Henry Thoreau) would eulogize their grandfather William Ellery as one of the many "who exercise an important influence within a limited sphere, in a thousand nameless ways," who communicate some "invisible virtue . . . without a distinct consciousness of it, on their own part, or that of others."[6] Both brothers speak through a deeply tired nostalgia. Whereas Emerson would seek (in the same year as Edward's homage to his grandfather) to throw off the "sepulchral" weight of the past, the Channings seek rather desperately to rehabilitate their father's generation—to dignify it, to salvage its decency and worth. They speak not in cocky American accents but in the elegiac tones of Victorian, feminine England, where "the effect of [a] being" could be "incalculably diffusive," and the truest heroes those who lived "faithfully a hidden life."[7] Occasionally the renovation yields hardy pioneers: "How little is thought in this lucifer-match age, of the hard times of our progenitors, especially on a winter morning, when they were compelled, with tinder-box between their knees . . . to catch a spark."[8] The dilemma of living between an American past that the imagination must recast and a future indifferent to the task is one of the central problems for Channing's generation.

Like his father and grandfather, William Channing senior made his living from Newport's commerce, but unlike them he took a law degree and preferred to depend on perpetual litigation—a well not likely to dry up in Newport. His legal practice was not always straightforward: one letter to a young woman advises her to sidestep her pursuing husband in order not to jeopardize her suit for divorce on grounds of desertion. But Channing had many claims to dignity. Of proper lineage, he had been sent to Princeton, where, a student of John Witherspoon and a friend of Samuel Stanhope Smith, he earned no academic distinction but enjoyed his years well enough to consider sending his son there. (Young Channing would, in the end, go to Harvard—"received," in the words of his mother's father, who seemed to regard it as something of a rescue, "into the bosom of my Alma Mater."[9]) The elder William entertained George Washington at his table—a sufficient, if not sumptuous, table. His house had two gardens to stock its kitchen, both tended by the family's domestic slaves—turned servants after the Revolutionary War. A good lawyer, Channing had no shortage of clients; failing or thriving, traders needed counsel. His logic held: since the economy of the seaport rested on the toil of West Indian slaves and the thirst of New Englanders, business was reliable. But Channing never amassed much of a fortune and the family lived with a mild variability. When John Jay and other seasoned Federalists followed Washington to their table, the family could surpass its daily station, but it was a bit, just a bit, of a strain.

All things considered, Channing preferred the reliability of law to the risks of business; his family had not been unfamiliar with burdensome debt, even ruin. Financial health was his measure of vitality: "The Arrival of the [French] Fleet & Army hath given new Life to the Town. There is more Business transacting and money circulating than formerly."[10] Such a Newport life did not allow—and Channing did not wish—a scrupulous selectivity in business or social contact. Involvement with the substantial Jewish community was inevitable; Aaron Lopez, of one of the oldest Sephardic families in America, had been the confidante of the financially troubled Channings earlier in the century, and a "kinsman" of Lopez would keep the books of Gibbs and Channing until the dissolution of the firm. When the family church suffered damage in the war, it seemed natural to William to borrow Touro synagogue, which had survived the British siege. It was all arranged until Ezra Stiles objected.[11] No less than his sons, Channing observed only loose boundaries between denominations; instrumental in arranging the lease of Trinity property for building a ropewalk, he marched with the rest of Newport's notables in an Anglican memorial procession for General Washington, serving as honorary pallbearer.[12] Exchange between competitive clergy and congregants, even on less ecumenical occasions, was always free and easy. It was not a town of sharply exclusive convictions.

"Agreeable and much disposed to social intercourse," Channing hardly chafed against the congenial ways of Newport. One thing, however, inflamed him: "He had a deep, I may say peculiar abhorrence of the vice of prophaneness," his son recalled, under the fear of which the younger William grew up pure-spoken in a blaspheming city.[13] But the son did not fully trust his father's sanitized speech. On the contrary, one of the few incidents he distinctly remembers is his father's outburst, on a day when the boy had accompanied him to court, against the opposing counsel for speaking indecorously. It so frightened the child to hear the usually "mellifluous" tones violated that he ran from the courthouse in terror. The father's propriety could be obsessive; his fastidiousness extended, in his son's recollection, to surfaces only. A benefactor to the church, his zeal was stirred by the need for renovation on the building, and he was diligent in observing the formalities. William Ellery Channing's homage to his father is strikingly, sadly spare. And it is so beyond the explanation that he almost sheepishly offers—that his father died when he was thirteen. Not a perfunctory, but a wistful respect touches his imperfect recollections: "I . . . am . . . desirous," he writes, while confessing his incapacity to build it, "that there should be some memorial to him."[14]

And yet there does exist, in the growth of Channing's mind, such a memorial. It is a memorial of instruction by negative example. The relation is not one of active dislike or energizing antagonism but rather a regretful alienation from the father's superficial respectability. Channing perceives in his father's life a falling short of congruence between expression and conviction—in the spoken pieties, in the zeal for externals, in the call for purer language without commensurate gain in the nature of its content. Around the edges of these memories lies the tinge of a father's hypocrisy.

But most fundamental—and a richly illuminating interpretation of his own past—is Channing's sorrow, articulated less than a year before he died, at his father's tolerance of slavery. This is the greatest indictment of his father's moral sense; it rings with deep self-reference, and it raises the unnegotiable standard that Channing would hold up—not always consciously—throughout his life. "My father," he writes, "had no sensibility of the evil."[15] He is lamenting not a particular blindness but a constitutional inability to recognize heinous sin.

Deprived early of this troubling father, who had held aloof from the boy from the start and who died in 1793, William became a grandfather's son. William Ellery lived to ninety-two and made his presence felt in the formative years of his namesake; his vitality and freshness belie the stale terms—"bedrock," "mainstay"—with which Channing biographies have usually characterized his relationship to his community. In fact he was a prickly, bull-headed man, not always in harmony with Newport's respectables. "Physicians some times Gild the Pills which they administer to Females," he wrote to his favorite grandson, "but I am neither a gilder nor a dauber."[16] Another grandson recalls the sarcasm with which he rebuked the well-to-do merchants who chatted outside the church and, entering, interrupted the prayer: "The effect of his words was magical; there was no further disturbance."[17] Ellery's long life yields a story—more than a patchwork of such anecdotes—of real urgency in its questioning of social assumptions. It was partly through his influence that his grandson began to turn inward, and at an early age into a questioning posture.

"He bore the marks," wrote still another grandson, "of habitual self-inspection."[18] What emerges from the documents he left is a man for whom the filiopious description rings true: sensitive to pride and uncomfortable with his own impetuosity, Ellery pushed himself toward humility; above all, he pulled back from the undiscriminating praise of others, confessing (and it was a confession, not self-praise) to know himself better than his admirers knew him. One of the few Federalists whom Jefferson retained in office (he was a signer of the Declaration), he gritted his teeth and performed his tasks as Newport customs collector even during the Embargo, 'a measure which he at heart repudiated."[19] He often felt the opposing pulls of duty and conviction, of local and national loyalty. A man "in moral warfare" with himself, he was aware that even his first embrace of revolutionary principles—joining the Sons of Liberty—had followed quickly on the heels of the threat to business posed by the nonimportation agreements. Neither burning for rebellion then nor committed later to blockade, he more than once found his actions and motives out of joint; he felt it, and he said it. In the process "he drew the young to him . . . and they felt they owed to him . . . in no small degree, the direction and coloring of their thoughts." To the grandson named after him he communicated two questions that would linger: What is finally the relation between motive and act? And to what degree is a man responsible for comprehending his own motives? Edward Tyrrel Channing supplied Ellery's undogmatic response: he was a man "anxious for the certainty [of] truth."[20]

The best short way into Ellery's mind is through a diary he kept on a journey to Philadelphia in 1777. Heady, confident, he was riding to charter a nation; en route he kept an almost picaresque journal filled with drunken innkeepers and their daughters, revealing a various appetite and an appealing knack for self-mockery: "This Day had a confirmation of the glorious News of the Surrendry of the Col. of the Queens light Dragoons [General Burgoyne] with his whole Army. Learn hence proud Mortals the ignominious End of the vain Boaster!" Its highlight is an account of a stay at a roadside inn whose keeper, in "a doleful Pickle," warns that the road is crawling with "Tories and Horsestealers." Ellery and his companion barricade the windows and keep watch, wary of ambush, achingly alert. Then the ominous question comes: "in a tremulous Voice: what Noise is that? I listened and soon discovered that the Noise was occasioned by some Rats gnawing the Head of a bread Cask."[21] What makes this a provocative document for understanding Channing's origins is the exuberance of which it marks the end. For the significance of Ellery's subsequent political career, of which Channing heard much, lies in its growing distance from this kind of energy and self-deflating wit. Ellery vividly illustrates the young country's postrevolutionary malaise. "We mounted our Rozinantes," he can cheerfully say of his Philadelphia journey, laughing at the sobriety of revolution; the war of independence is still a slapstick skirmish.

Soon his tone changes. The clownish enemy becomes "barbarous," "implacable." Ellery's letters to a succession of Rhode Island governors convey his fatigue at the legislative haggling. "I am obliged," he writes in 1778, "to observe a . . . wearisome punctuality," and later, afflicted with headache and cold, he complains that "constant attendance without any opportunity of exercise is too much for humanity." As the letters move into the 1780s they darken with an awareness of discord: "the unsettled state of congress" grows more so every session; self and sectional interests begin to offend; he takes bitter note of "a vile, sordid practice of monopolizing, which some wealthy men here have got into."[22] Protesting his inability to represent Rhode Island singlehandedly, Ellery at last acquired a colleague, but by 1783 the new delegate, David Howell, had been censured by the Congress; the embarrassment and rancor spilled on to Ellery himself. A dispute over the legitimacy of their seats had grown out of their opposition to the impost—a duty on imports that would aid in raising revenue. Resentment rose against Howell, who had unsubtly appealed to latent North-South suspicion. The dispute finally ended with an insulting resolution, introduced by Virginia and seconded by South Carolina, effectively reducing the status of Howell and Ellery by calling for nullification of their votes in cases where they might be decisive.[23]

William Ellery had come to Congress a zealous and good-humored patriot; he left a sober, if not a bitter man. His patriotism cost him "all his destructible property"—the British looted and burned his Newport home. Now, with little humor left, he demands "some Tory habitation" to shelter himself upon his return. Half accepting, half rejecting a Rhode Island judgeship, he grumbles at the inadequate salary and solicits funds from home to avoid "the disgraceful necessity of leaving . . . indebted to the person with whom I have boarded."[24]

When he returned to his family, now augmented by a grandson, Ellery had changed; he had seen and participated in the beginnings of sectional strife, finding the interest of his state opposed to the interest of his nation. He had heard the Congress debate his expulsion on grounds that bore little relation to their real motives for expelling him.[25] He had seen the flush of independence dim more than a little. This excursion into his revolutionary experience is more than a corrective to the notion that he possessed unimpeachable patriotic credentials, for the figure of William Ellery looms large in the early years of his namesake; he took a special, almost proprietary interest in the boy, instructing him repeatedly in the dangers of gullibility and excess, in the fragility of union when a common enemy has passed, and in the perils of the national adventure. And perhaps his most fundamental lesson—one that would always inform the thought of his grandson—would be that "we ought to guard against our internal as well as external enemies."[26]

Ellery's daughter Lucy married William Channing in 1773 and bore ten children, seven of whom were sons. Petite and intermittently ill, she had the kind of moral authority that—through the example of vigor reached at risk to a delicate constitution—shames resistance. When Lucy Ellery shook with indignation, as she was known to do, the cause of her distress (whether a disobedient child or a dishonest shopkeeper) would feel the guilt of a self-conscious bully. She could make people feel small.

"Deeply offended by paltry equivocation," Mrs. Channing left on her sons not the father's imprint of a practiced sternness but the deeper influence of a temperament alert to duplicity.[27] Or at least this is the image into which her sons coaxed her memory. "I cannot recall one word or action betraying the slightest insincerity," Channing wrote after her death.[28] It is an oddly negative way of phrasing his praise, even for a man whose sentences often strain for the Addisonian ring and avoid, as an aesthetic indiscretion, the blunt and direct. The idea he is circling —the quality of sincerity—is crucial to Channing's recollection of his childhood, and it always centers on his mother.

Speaking in nearly choral unanimity, the Channings agree on Lucy Ellery's righteousness: "If pretension and fraud, in any of their manifold disguises, crossed her path, she became chillingly reserved."[29] This chilly integrity is a key to the mind of her son. For all his life he would feel himself hounded by voices of duplicity, and his darkest moments would come when he heard such a voice within. In effect, Channing's entire intellectual career can be read as an effort to fulfill the ideal that he and his brothers personified in their mother. Almost directly contrasted with the father, she embodies for her sons precisely those virtues which their father only mimics: the clarity of her vision pierces the Newport fog. The grandfather's moral self-awareness rises to high pitch in his daughter; indeed the significance of her image is its effectual transformation of moral insight from the field of human activity—politics, business, law, war—to the salon of domestic tranquillity. There are no tests of her fortitude in the hagiography of her sons; no hard choice of state versus nation, no divorce cases where feigned desertion may be a decent expedient as well as a conscious lie. She was, in short, a professional conscience, a woman with leisure to judge.

The accuracy of this portrait is a moot if interesting question. What must be carefully defined, however, is the nature of the need which compelled her most famous son to depict her as he did. One of the needs she satisfied was to show the way to a quiet haven away from the din of daily life, a place where moral choices were clear, where the older, spectator stance could survive in a world that demanded more and more participation. According to a recent study, such escape was the hallmark of Channing's generation.[30] Certainly for Channing himself it was a lifelong temptation. What makes Channing interesting is that for him it was not always a guarantor, but sometimes a subverter of honor. The world still called.

Lucy Channing took a direct and nervous hand in the nurture of her children. Channing's biographers have repeated with unspecific insinuations that he alone heeded his mother's command not to swim without supervision. His brothers broke the rule and developed competent strokes, while William watched from the beach. The anecdote is neatly suggestive—perhaps reason enough to dismiss it—but it is interestingly echoed in this backward glance to a generative childhood moment: "No spot on earth has helped to form me so much as that beach. There I lifted up my voice in praise amidst the tempest. There, softened by beauty, I poured my thanksgiving and contrite confessions. There, in reverential sympathy with the mighty power around me, I became conscious of the power within."[31] William Channing's first sensation of "the power within" is not a trivial event in the history of the American mind. Whether precisely remembered or fuzzily projected, it is the genesis of a faith whose first serene and unwavering spokesman he is often accounted to be. It is therefore worth weighing the possibility that Channing's conviction of man's share in the general divinity may be informed— not only in his retrospective imagination—by an unconfessed incapacity. The sea and the man—the *not-me* and the *me* in Emersonian terms—had never really met, and if they had, the man would, he knew, have drowned.

He knew that he had been a pampered child. As Channing himself is the source of much of the evidence that he was cod-

dled, his candor has something of the flavor of absolution. That
he was carried to "dame's school" in the arms of a Negro servant
hardly fuels his pride; that he was called "little minister" raises
the image of a child preciously imitating his mother, who habit-
ually called the children in for scripture reading and psalm sing-
ing (one room of the many-roomed house was set aside for these
sessions). The boy was known to thump on a warming-pan and
summon the servants to meeting, over which he would preside
and preach.

To a man so repelled by hollow convention, so sensitive to
posturing, his own childhood was an embarrassing progression
of sham performances. And so the man's analysis of the child's
opportunism yields, at best, a gray and melancholy picture of
Newport days. It yields not only this sense of complicity in an
amoral routine, but also a significantly ambivalent picture of the
child's constant model: woman. Channing recalls the ritual of
the schoolroom: "When we entered the door we kissed our
hands, and Madam was the first word which escaped our lips."[32]
The teacher's "title was *Madam*," and though any other name
escapes him, she calls up an image that encompasses Channing's
idea of a half-century's feminine history: "She sat in a large easy
chair, and, unlike the insect forms of modern days, she filled the
capacious seat." How much disgust he invests in the adjectival
"insect" is a risky speculation; but whether it is a metaphor for
small-waisted, leggy ladies or a character description, it illuminates rather sharply Channing's preference for the old to the
"modern" female. Fond nostalgia for the battle-ax schoolmarm is
a common enough emotion, but the intensity of the contrast is a
little less common, and it raises the possibility that resentment
accompanies his deference to women. To belittle the schoolmarm's scrawny descendant is perhaps a strategy for proving
that he was in tow to real women, not insects.

Channing saw himself as his mother's boy, inheriting her
sickliness and her public piety. Recollected by an "aged rela-

tive," it seems to have been so from the beginning: "Standing by
the mother's side . . . [he had] brilliant eyes, glowing cheeks,
and light brown hair falling in curls upon his shoulders, dressed
in a green velvet jacket, with ruffled collar and white under-
clothes."[33] That the "unhappy influences"[34] of his Newport
childhood might have included his mother is less readily inferred
from his conscious memoirs, but it is worth noting that the devoted son who earned his grandfather's praise—"Your letters
have afforded me great delight, for they have all discovered that
affectionate regard for your mother"—would, soon after, incur
his disappointment—"Your Ma and I and all your relations take
it very unkindly that you have not favored one of us at least
with a letter during the vacation . . . P.S. I shall expect an answer very soon." Rather than constituting interrupted speech,
the early letters from Cambridge seem to punctuate a silence,
leaving Ellery discomforted if not disturbed, always asking for
more. William Henry marks a tension that may have caused
these silences by emphasizing the blustery boy who "was a remarkable wrestler, [and] excelled in pitching the quoit," but who
softened to a curly-haired angel under the influence of the
hearth. If "his first feeling of the sacredness of woman was called
out by observing that the delicate hands of the girls at school
were never marked by the ferule," it may have been a reflexive
reverence: "I wish in my heart you were like William Channing,"
the teacher would exclaim at the class brat. William's hands were
hardly scarred.[35]

Channing, in sum, lived a suppressed boyhood—if not
emasculated, at least intimidated. He was instructed in the perils
of energy and embarrassed by his own sanctimony. At twelve, a
year before his father's death, he was sent to Connecticut to his
paternal uncle, with whom he would prepare for Harvard. New
London and Cambridge would be the scenes of his first en-
counters with himself: the places where he would rethink, or
think through for the first time, the nature of his heritage. What

is finally moving about the growth of child into man is the degree to which he surmounted the preciousness without bile, his success in coming to terms with his constituted gentleness. He would not lapse into misogyny or self-indulgent chest-baring, as would Thoreau or Francis Parkman, who detested Channing "for his meager proportions, sedentary habits, environment of close air and female parishioners."[36] Nor would he sink into breast-beating and saccharine gentility as would so many of his peers. His achievement is attested by his ability to hold clearly in mind a distinction between gentility and gentleness. Only an inner strength can admit this sympathy without shame:

> I found a nest of birds in my father's field, which held four young ones. They had no down when I first discovered them. They opened their little mouths as if they were hungry, and I gave them some crumbs which were in my pocket. Every day I returned to feed them . . . They were now feathered and ready to fly. When I came one morning, I found them all cut up into quarters. The grass round the nest was red with blood. Their little limbs were raw and bloody. The mother was on a tree, and the father on the wall, mourning for their young . . . I thought, too, that the parents looked on me as the author of their miseries, and this made me still more unhappy. I wanted to undeceive them . . . When I left the field, they followed me with their eyes and with mournful reproaches. I was too young and too sincere in my grief to make any apostrophes . . . I cried . . . for I was a child.[37]

"A man booted and with a horsewhip in hand" was the image left by Channing's Connecticut uncle on one quaking Yale freshman. "At the end of the year," the student recalls, "Mr. Tutor Channing . . . left, with which I was well pleased."[38] Henry Channing was on his way to New London; he left behind the taste of severity not only on students—who had tried to beat down his door in the spring disorders of 1786—but also on Ezra Stiles himself. "He . . . wants," regretted the Yale president, "the Mansuetude & Wattsian sweetness of Manners."[39] Depending on the source of the report, this Channing was a stern or glowering character, but no one accounts him sweet. His letters can display a grating sarcasm: "The Paper money gentry considered me as greatly reprehensible because, when at Newport, I publicly prayed for and pitied them"; but he can also be disarmingly self-aware, in this case on his hot courtship: "It has long been supposed that I could not be at Lyme without being—you know where. And the supposition was generally just."[40] Despite his social failings, Channing earned respect; Stiles had once considered that he might be the sorely needed man "to bear away the Palm" of Jonathan Edwards. It seemed less likely when he appeared to doubt "the eternal generation of the son," yet six years later he was still a serious candidate for the vacant professorship of divinity.[41]

Henry Channing came to New London to preach at a grisly occasion. A twelve-year-old Pequot girl, enraged by an accusation that she had pilfered strawberries, had strangled her six-year-old accuser and smashed her head with stones. Channing preached before the hanging. He harangued the guilty girl in the presence of her victim's coffin: "Is this prisoner then condemned? So is the unbeliever." And he left little doubt that he had in mind some of the town respectables: "What then can we think of those who rise up early and sit up late and eat the bread of carefulness that they may leave an inheritance to their children while the provision for their minds is scarcely thought of?"[42] This bristling tone dominates the sermon, which improves the occasion as God's solicitation to tend the wayward children. It is a hymn to education, but a cantankerous one; indeed the whole business has an air of the macabre about it, with the terrified condemned girl looking on as the minister lectures negligent parents. (Her father was unknown and her mother executed long before for abandoning her.) In any case, Henry Channing swept into New London on a wave of admonition—and the admonished apparently liked it. He shortly began a seventeen-year ministry, succeeding the same William Patten who had chilled the Channings in Newport.

This first sermon conforms to the structure and intent of the classic jeremiad, with a small but important sociological difference: it is spoken not in the face of economic or social calamity but amid the uneasiness of a fragile prosperity in a town growing three times faster than the state. It is a prescription for protection, not recovery, of the comfortable life, and yet it is essentially a document of declension, for it manages piety as a means to forestall such savage judgments as the murder. It warns against complacency, but not for the sake of saving the complacent soul, rather for the sake of security. The sermon illuminates the mental world into which young William Channing would be introduced under his uncle's tutelage, for the call that Henry answered to fill the New London pulpit was not the warm plea of flock to shepherd that the Channing biographers have assumed; it was, in fact, a tough-minded contract that kept him there through years of squabbling over salary and doctrine. The basis for Henry Channing's ministry was the conventional need for an articulate conscience, and, as in all instances where one party is charged with prescriptive moral criticism of another, the union was not a happy one.

What young William encountered was not a minister exhorting revival but a man half-contemptuous of his congregants and a town increasingly suspicious of their minister.[43] He liked his uncle. Indeed, Henry Channing seemed to serve a purpose of reassurance, matching and echoing the boy's doubts about Newport life. "A truly wretched people," he called the Rhode Island assemblymen.[44] Even his public utterances suggest a self-consciousness that the younger Channing could recognize: "My soul shudders at the recollection of the horrid expressions of cursing and blasphemy, with which the virtuous ear is often pained— I dare not repeat them—should I attempt it . . . its touch should leave me unclean."[45] A lasting concord grew up between them: "Always with you our hearts were made glad—We never can forget such a nephew, or rather such a son." "You know," replies William, "that it would constitute the happiest circumstances of my life to contribute to your happiness."[46] Their mutual sympathy seems to have flourished in a shared impatience with the pressure of community.

It is not clear, when pew-rentals were raised and communion tankards replaced by silver cups, who initiated the changes. Perhaps to teach their minister frugality, the church committee became more and more tight-fisted toward him, granting yearly bonuses but never a rise in salary. The letters between them move from cool to icy; behind the financial pressure seems to be a dissatisfaction with his preaching. It is difficult to determine precisely the nature of the falling-out. Doubtless Channing's unseemly defense of an avowedly Unitarian minister from a neighboring town and his generally relaxed doctrines are near the heart of the matter.[47] But one senses at work here something closer to mutual embarrassment than to spiritual conflict, as if the tacit understanding that the ministry should whip up community guilt—as he had so splendidly done on the execution day —has been violated. It is possible to construe the New London years as evidence that Channing's uncle was a muddle-headed man, opportunistic, without steadiness of purpose. Henry's letters do reveal a streak of cynicism. And yet it is also possible to feel a moral turmoil in him. From his conviction that "We have here striking evidence of the depravity of human nature," he moves, at risk to his position, toward a more liberal stance.[48] One night a parishioner went with handbill, hammer, and nail to a public signpost in the town. Next morning the citizens could read, "Mr. Henry Channing, we agreed with you to preach Jesus Christ, not John Adams, in that most Holy Place, I mean the pulpit."[49] That "pulpit was overshadowed by a sound-board of apparently terrific weight, which was sustained by an iron rod, undoubtedly of great strength, but not of sufficient size to dissipate all anxiety from the minds of beholders."[50] Some were developing mixed feelings about its stability.

It was the beginning of the end. Like a dead marriage, the

relation wound on, and when Channing finally interpreted the committee's silence as an expectation that he would resign, he wrote a bitter and moving letter. "You have not complained of [your minister's] sensibility when his heart has melted under your sorrows; and can you ask him to be indifferent to his own? . . . Often I have gone, with my life in my hands, to minister to the sick and the dying, and to bind up the broken-hearted . . . possibly you may think it your unhappiness to have a Minister who feels too much."[51] The value of his pastorate had outweighed his heresy for more than a decade.[52] Both sides in the controversy knew he had betrayed an old ideal, but neither could really understand it; without the old religion Channing still graced his pastoral office, and he ought not—he pleaded— to have been pilloried. His nephew probably saw no more than the seeds of this drama (though they kept in constant touch), but the intimacy that grew up between them contains a shared confusion. The younger Channing would inwardly quarrel with his own conventional parishioners, and the Baltimore sermon in which he would declare his Unitarianism in 1819 has a precedent in this New London apostasy.

Not yet fifteen, Channing was the youngest member of the class that assembled in Harvard Yard in September 1794 to hear the Hollis Professor welcome them formally to college. The professor, David Tappan, took the occasion to scold in advance of transgression. If the freshmen were listening, and if they expected a high-sounding charge, they were due for surprise. More pleading than stirring, his sermon speaks a plaintive language: "Let me beseech you to make [God] a present and operative reality in your minds." Almost embarrassed by the vitiated summons to piety, Tappan alternates between plea and threat; he promises disaster "if they wage war upon the unoffending and beautiful works of art which commode and adorn these magnificent buildings." All in all, it is a defensive performance. And yet, nine years later Channing would ask Tappan (after Uncle Henry declined) to deliver the sermon at his Boston ordination, and the professor would again solicit gentleness from his audience—this time to honor not fragile paintings but the delicate health of their young minister.[53]

There is a kind of historical neatness to Tappan's presiding presence at these two occasions. Through him one hears again the languid melancholy that was so much a part of the mental universe into which Channing was born: "You will consider . . . that the honor of this ancient seminary is in a serious sense confided to your care."[54] There is a flabbiness here, a surrender to mutability, for Tappan conceives a total separation between institution and members; his calling has shriveled to a constabulary function—to protect the college from transients. He bespeaks not a real sense of history, but a sentiment of aimlessness, an idea of static form in permanent opposition to energy, with no imagined fusion. It was a central failing of New England culture in the first third of the new century (if not perennially since), and New England's restless minds knew it.[55] This, at the least, was a disheartened Harvard, and Tappan—described by enemies as "reluctant to suggest an opinion, which did not meet the approbation of others"—spoke for his university.[56]

Evidently a general solicitousness extended downward from the Hollis Professor through the faculty ranks; the son of President Willard reports that if a "Tutor was convinced that he was exacting too much, he would listen . . . and redress the grievance." Faculty patience was tried daily; "The taking of notes I do not remember ever to have seen practiced."[57] In this atmosphere of hesitant education, Channing was an exemplary student. Finishing first in his class, he shunned wine, incurred fines only for absence due to illness, and rarely participated in the revels of the Porcellian and Hasty Pudding Clubs, which elected him to membership. He willingly obeyed his grandfather's warning to "pay no regard to the smart, adroit, caricaturists at college."[58]

The Speaking Club was another matter, for much of his energy in the first two years went toward the development of oral power; he read Longinus, Sheridan on elocution, a biography of Demosthenes, Cicero, and Shakespeare. And soon he earned a reputation for eloquence. Joseph Story even quotes Milton's account of Adam enraptured by Raphael to signify Channing's effect on his hearers.[59] From the bloodless preaching of Newport to the animated rage of his uncle, Channing had been sensitive to a range of rhetorical possibility, and his first goal at Harvard—even before he knew his vocation—was to teach himself to speak. A surviving undergraduate oration on Jacobinism shows a conventional grandiloquence and sophomoric fervor, but it leaves no doubt which end of the rhetorical spectrum he was aiming for. It was another form of valediction to his Newport childhood.

Cambridge, however, did not see an end to the precious insularity of that childhood. He lodged not in student rooms but in one of the grand mansions of the city, the estate of Francis Dana (the companion of his grandfather's Philadelphia jaunt), who had married his mother's sister. By the time Channing arrived, Dana had completed his long diplomatic career and was Chief Justice of Massachusetts. He made a "spontaneous offer" to pay his nephew's expenses,[60] which the Channings gratefully accepted. Always inclined toward diplomacy, Dana had failed more than succeeded. Traveling to England in 1775 to promote amity, he had sought some mutually agreeable form of independence. Spurned, he had stood in 1776 at Valley Forge with Washington against a suspicious Congress. The General found him a valuable ally because of the range of those who trusted him; John Adams and Sam Adams both called him friend. After the war, with John Quincy Adams, who called him a second father, he carried American credentials to the court of Catherine the Great, who would not receive an envoy of revolution. The empress made them wait for two years in St. Petersburg before sending them home. There was, then, a certain battered noblesse about the judge (his brother had married the daughter of an English lord), and through him Channing was exposed to another form of gentility in retreat from an increasingly raw culture.

Dana fell nearly into ruin when one of his sons invested heavily in the piers of Cambridgeport, over which the mansion had a commanding view. When the port failed, the servants were dismissed, and soon Dana's daughters were actually doing housework. (Eventually the house would be home to a family named Fuller, which included an energetic daughter called Margaret.) Slowly Dana "seems to have withdrawn into a mysterious twilight of invalidism. A slender figure, wrapped in his Russian furs, he was still occasionally seen in the streets of Cambridge."[61] From this house that reeked of the past, young Channing took his daily walk to a college that enshrined the past. Even his plucky grandfather showed signs of bewilderment before the new times; he writes a touching letter to William at the start of the second term in 1797: "The ideas I have received from reading . . . are so impertinent that although I kick them out they will return and plague me with their visits. If I had as good a command over them as the good Centurion had over his soldiers, it would be more tolerable; but when I tell them to go they wont budge, and there is no getting rid of some of them without . . . throwing everything into confusion."[62] It is all the more remarkable that in this world of apologetic teachers and dwindling privilege, a world in which "grace" had completed the shift from its seventeenth- to its eighteenth-century meaning, Channing had a light, if not a fire, that stirred his peers.[63] Every push that he would make toward a more vital piety, toward a reconciliation of form and energy, toward a more fluid politics, would be made against this heritage.

In his junior year Channing's reading ranged from tracts on rhetoric to speculations on the nature of man. He borrowed

Richard Price, Rousseau, Cervantes, Joseph Priestley, and, with special eagerness, Francis Hutcheson's *Inquiry into the Originals of our Ideas of Beauty and Virtue* (1725). It is not clear whether he read Edwards's *Nature of True Virtue* (1758) at this time—he did read the *Enquiry into the Freedom of the Will* (1754) and a few months later, the sermons of Edwards's great disciple, Samuel Davies[64]—but he had what his biographers have called an Edwardsean conversion under the spell of Hutcheson. "I longed to die and felt as if heaven alone could give room for the exercise of such emotion."[65] What Channing found in Hutcheson was a confirmation of his own instinct to associate aesthetic harmony with virtue and discord with sin. Lying, in his childhood world, had been branded an ugly thing. Hutcheson helped him also to formulate a reply to the Newport and Harvard experiences of divided sensibility, where in the rhythms of everyday living ideals and actions were given up as hopelessly sundered. (Tappan's ideal for Harvard students was to have them "complete their collegiate course without incurring the least stain upon their reputation.")[66] One suspects that the bond with Uncle Henry grew from the same need that Hutcheson filled, from an apprehension of unity in perception and act; it was a comforting fact that Henry Channing's commitment to his pastoral duty survived the cooling of his orthodox ardor. The secular vocabulary of Hutcheson, who was tried by the Glasgow Presbytery for teaching "that it is possible to have a knowledge of good and evil without, and prior to, a knowledge of God," was similarly comforting.[67] Less a hindrance than an aid to Channing's assent, it opened an avenue to the ministry by sweeping away doctrinal issues. The spirit of benevolence had now become the one thing needful.

Channing found in Hutcheson an idea of disinterested benevolence that he would meet again through Samuel Hopkins in Newport, and which would now grow into a program for his life. He continued to contemplate law and medicine (his grandfather sent him lists of medical textbooks as late as November 1796), but finally he settled on the ministry. He could, with the sanction of Hutcheson, conceive all three as branches of one endeavor. The law, in its associations with his father's Newport, could seem potentially subversive of the selfless aim, and medicine simply would not exercise his gifts. It was, then, the ministry, not exactly by default but because it fit a constellation of moral assumptions that preceded the choice. It was, in effect, the logical thing to do.

"I am most cheerful when I am most religious," Channing confided to a friend in the fall of 1798.[68] Hutcheson sanctioned such statements as this by obliterating the distinction between self-interest and altruism. Here was a way of meeting the needs of the self and tending the needs of others, but the identity, or the balance, would not always remain so obvious. For this reason it is important to see how a vision of spiritual cooperation governed the start of Channing's career. In coming years when he felt himself aloof, or when he found violent discord among those who appealed for his support, he would be shaken to the foundations of his work, if not his life. Hutcheson could ridicule the idea of rational computation of advantages as the anatomy of choice by calling it an unwieldy process, "endless toil" that could not explain the instant motions of the will.[69] This refreshing common sense was precious to Channing, but he would have to fight to keep his faith in it. For finally Francis Hutcheson had moved him because he combated those who held "that all the desires of the human mind . . . are reducible to self-love."[70] And yet the history of Channing's ministry was a grim and slow accommodation to the universal—or at least the national—triumph of self-love.

Channing's discovery of Hutcheson reinvigorated another of his purposes: "Being then but fifteen, turning strongly to the female sex, I considered that they were the powers which ruled the world, and that, if they would bestow their favor on the right cause only, and never be diverted by caprice, all would be fitly arranged, and triumph was sure."[71] The newly strengthened identity of beauty and virtue allowed this explicit hymn to femininity, the seeds of which were present in his Newport relations, especially in his emulation of his mother. But the conditional phrase, "if . . . the right cause," represents a serious demurral, an implicit speculation on the volatile caprice of woman. A love poem to constancy, its adolescent pitch can only be reached with inconstancy in mind. In short, it is shrill in its praise because it is wary of the worthiness of the praised. The reminiscence shows Channing in a characteristic mental operation—channeling vital (in this case sexual) energy into virtuous pathways.

At the same time that he was deifying the temperate woman, the undergraduate Channing shook his fist at the Jacobins: "We have seen a nation in Europe grasping . . . trampling . . . systematizing rapine and plunder." Though standard, this rhetoric also facilitates insight into the young man's psychological state through its inauthentic self-image: "We were not the sons of those who sealed our liberties with their blood if we would not now defend with these lives that soil which affords a peaceful grave to the mouldering bones of our forefathers."[72] As an upperclassman, Channing grew louder and louder in his Federalist pride; indeed Joseph Stevens Buckminster remembered the diatribe against France as having been delivered with a characteristic "nervous expression."[73] Mindful of previous disorders, the college authorities tried to dampen the invective of Channing's senior oration. The young patriot threatened to refuse his degree (one classmate did), but finally a compromised wording was reached. Still, the biggest ovation of the day came with Channing's rebuking sentence: "But that I am forbid, I could a tale unfold, which would harrow up your souls."[74] Whether Channing recalled the episode as childish sulking or as vindication of principle, it remains curious in its celebration of the filiopious theme, for the fact is—and Channing knew it well—that *his* fathers had spilled no blood and precious few tears in the dark days of the revolution. It is true enough that his father had applauded at Rhode Island's adoption of the constitution, but he, like his brother Henry and his father-in-law—indeed all of Channing's "fathers"—had recoiled from the more fundamental revolutionary energies that independence released. In short, Channing's later Harvard years find him struggling to link himself to a line of heroic rebels who simply did not exist. To make them seem real, he had to construe vested-interest conservatism as high idealism. It was exactly the kind of self-deception he would come to detest. Channing left Harvard with a vocation, an exercised gift for oratory, and a noisy commitment to a reasonable revolution, which he had neither experienced nor honestly understood. In coming years he would meet many men who roughly shared those characteristics. He would distrust them, even dislike them.

In November 1798, after a restless summer at home, Channing sailed for Virginia to assume the position of tutor to the children of David Randolph, a Richmond gentleman who had summered in Newport and been impressed with the young man. Their meeting proved consequential, for in Richmond Channing would close—with some struggle—his adolescence and confront a more than histrionic responsibility in the world. In this period, spanning less than two years, the fundamental themes of his thought would become fully recognizable. They did not emerge without pain.

The Randolph children owned his days but not his evenings, and he became jealous of his time. At first enchanted with the Richmond social life, he deferred to Southern charm even to the point of embarrassing self-denigration: "How different from our Northern manners . . . I blush for my own people when I compare the selfish prudence of a Yankee with the generous confidence of a Virginian."[75] But soon he absented himself from the well-lubricated gatherings, moving rather abruptly from chandelier to simple candlelight, studying late in an unheated outbuilding, spending the money from home only on books. He allowed his clothes to fray and grow threadbare and used them as an excuse to avoid the parties. The sharp swing from the sociable to the insular is characteristic of the Richmond years, which are full of violent self-chastisement: "I have suffered . . . from a painful sense of defects." Without a doubt, a guilty suppression of sexual impulse is working here. When he writes "could I only take from the Virginians their *sensuality*," he means extirpate, not borrow—but syntax is not the only sign that he found a mirror in the Virginians. (He was stunned, for one thing, by their powers of public speech.) His first biographer attributes the spartan regimen to the "end of overcoming effeminacy," but Channing himself is more candid: "some at this critical period abandon themselves to sensual excess."[76]

Channing abandoned himself to himself, and this retreat into solipsism triggered a self-loathing that even lust could not evoke. His grandfather's worries were baseless: "There is not an inviolable connection between tobacco and Grogg, but . . ."[77] He was flailing now, unwilling to let his body govern him, but equally disgusted with the retrenchment of his mind. In the crisis he articulated a rather desperate mind/body separation, a strategy to circumvent what he really knew to be an inseparable connection; such a separation never entirely disappears from his thought. He slept on the floor and woke freezing and walked before sunrise to forestall numbness in his limbs. His biographers have concluded from one letter that he now experienced periods of causeless weeping while scanning his books. Though credible, this seems an unjustified inference, for Channing did weep, but he wept for a reason. He was desperate for purpose. The aimlessness of Newport life, the predicament of the conscientious ministry, the feel of Harvard adrift—all the measures of his young life converged upon him now and sent him reeling. He wept for himself and wondered how to find direction. To his friend Shaw he wrote, "Do give me a recipe for curing this disorder."[78]

It is not possible to reconstruct exactly the steps to resolution. Seen from the new distance, home was losing its palpability—his letters fight to recall it. There was no rest to be found in the things for which he was growing homesick. It was in this sense that he moved out of adolescence; as childish as the crisis can seem, Channing was not fooled into thinking its resolution lay in past things. To regret their passing was no longer the same as imagining final solace in them. He had, after all, come beyond the rhetoric of his Harvard Commencement address.

Not unlike Teufelsdröckh, he begins to channel his violence against romantic egotism, against that part of him which was wallowing in self-pity. Indeed the Richmond period bears some resemblance to the Blumine episode of *Sartor Resartus*, that archetypal disintegration and recovery of the Victorian personality. There is even a rejecting woman, a shadowy figure who patronizes Channing in that most devastating way: something that he finds grand she calls pretty; something he reveres, she appreciates: "The other day, I handed to a lady a sonnet of Southey's, which had wrung tears from me. 'It is pretty,' said she, with a smile. 'Pretty!' echoed I, as I looked at her. 'Pretty!' I went home."[79] The process of Channing's reintegration may be described as the transformation of this kind of personal affront—the hurt administered by a world insensitive to fine feeling—into an intellectual position. He would, he declares, from now on no longer put his trust in feeling; he would act by a principle of duty, a sort of compulsion rather than inner light. Ultimately it amounts to a check on Hutcheson. And it is a turn away from voluntarism toward a kind of moral coercion, a turn he would never fully reverse.

The recovery from self-indulgence took several forms. It

seems at first to have pulled him from tolerance to discipline in
the management of his pupils; apparently he even came close to
whipping them, leading his grandfather to express the hope that
he would not resort to "flagellation [which] would probably
overthrow . . . that mutual confidence . . . that subsists between
you and your scholars." But more than a change of pedagogy,
there comes a change of heart, a change that Channing reports to
his uncle, perhaps as rejoinder to Henry's skepticism on the possibility of conversion. Scripture comes to dominate William's
reading now, and his grandfather no longer complains, as he did
to him at Harvard, that "among [your books] I do not recollect
that I saw that best of books, the Bible." On the contrary, his
grandson's new devoutness alarms Ellery far beyond a gentle-
manly concern for the well-being of the Randolph children: "I do
not altogether agree with you that the stake and faggot are more
favorable to the church, than liberty of conscience and the most
unlimited toleration . . . I have no notion at present of being
whipt or burnt into Religion."[80] The letters which elicited this
response are unfortunately lost, but it is clear enough that Channing is pulling back with some revulsion from the spirit of
watery-eyed benevolence that dignified his former languor. "It is
true . . . I weep over a novel. I weep over a tale of human woe.
But do I ever relieve the distressed? . . . I have found that virtue
does not consist in feeling, but in *acting from a sense of duty*."[81]

Channing was wavering in his high estimate of human nature, a faith whose sacred text remained Hutcheson's *Inquiry*.
With Napoleon very much on his mind, the dose of compas-
sionate humility that Hutcheson parceled out for every man
seemed eradicable to William now. (Though Napoleon's Italian
and Egyptian campaigns were going badly, by the summer of
1799 he was conspicuously moving toward total control of
France. The "Jacobin" menace had been confirmed.) Among the
weakest and most perfunctory sections of the *Inquiry* are those
which rationalize "the cruelties of the Nero's and Domitian's,"

those which explain crime as manifestations of a diseased moral sense, arguing that even the criminal tends to justify his acts on moral grounds.[82] Part of Channing's growth into maturity is a perception of radical evil in the world and of man's capacity to ignore it or to slake his conscience by deploring it. The real achievement of the Richmond years is Channing's increasingly resolute refusal to stand any longer on an easy externalization of evil. As one consequence of the maturing sense of the self's involvement in sin, he shed his political blinders—his tone softens on France and hardens on England. Not merely a prelude to their switching places as foe and friend, it is an acknowledgment of gray where only black and white had been before. Even in the nervous aftermath of the XYZ Affair, he opposes a standing army, and though he exclaims "Old England, forever!" at the news of Nelson's victory, he cautions, "I do not wish England to rise on [the] ruins of France."[83]

Undoubtedly the milieu of Jeffersonian Virginia had its effect in muting Channing's strident Federalism, but more than Republican rumbling (not much of which invaded the Randolph household), it was a new kind of Federalist that affected him. He applauded John Marshall for voting to repeal the Alien and Sedition Acts. In short, his sobered vision of human nature included a new component of sophistication. His regional identification had been called into question.

This greater suppleness of mind came hand in hand with new literary experiences: he read Mary Wollstonecraft, whom he thought "the greatest [woman] of the age," more Rousseau, and the French mystic Fénelon, and dashed off some almost hysterical letters calling for a pastoral communism to squelch the root of all evil, avarice.[84] One book had special force for him, Godwin's *Caleb Williams* (1794), a novel of faceless enemies and barely motivated malignity that not only fit his lonely Virginia mood but also showed him the brooding side of the great reformer. In *Political Justice* (1793) and *Caleb Williams*,

Channing found corollaries to his own hope and dread for the human future. The central plot of the novel takes its protagonist from benevolence to malevolence—a journey that Channing now found sadly plausible. As a recent critic has said, the book is not only an "object lesson in the corrigible faults of government" but also "a tragedy of the incorrigible division in the human mind."[85] Channing could feel both themes now.

He turned as well to biographies of monarchs; a growing interest in power, in the forceful personality so lacking in his New England experience, carried him through lives of Henry VII, George III, Louis XIV. Indeed the romance of power grew upon him; it even seeps into his reaction to the specter of slavery; he speaks more in indignation at the usurpation of power than in horror at indignity: "Man, when forced to substitute the will of another for his own, ceases to be a moral agent . . . No empire is so valuable as the empire of one's self. No right is so . . . necessary . . . as the right of exerting the powers which nature has given us."[86] This rhetoric is more than a little prophetic of the inner dynamic of Northern abolitionism and of Channing's half-participation in it.

His health broken, he asked the Randolphs to let him go and sailed for Newport on a coal-carrying sloop, which ran aground while her captain drank. Calm weather and a rising tide lifted her off the sand bar, and Channing arrived home to find a fretful family. His appearance—thin, hollow-eyed—was a shock; but not only his self-denial had changed him. He had seen dark things—in books, in his imagination, and in the reality of human slavery amid gentility and grace. But it would be a mistake to think he merely recoiled, for he also carried home a new insight and new eloquence. "You tell me," he wrote to his friend Shaw, "I am only a candle. Perhaps I am less—a farthing rushlight, a glowworm on a . . . shrub. You say I am discontented at not being the sun. No such thing! . . . Give me but the consciousness that I have done all I could and ought to do . . . Philosophers tell us that a candle fills with light a sphere of four miles' diameter. Send me the dimensions of your sphere. Mine is fifteen feet by ten. Is it not shameful!"[87] More truly alone in Richmond than he had ever been before, Channing achieved there something indispensable. He took upon himself the affliction of his fathers and his peers; he ceased railing at the world and turned instead to examine his own evasions, his strategies for eluding truths that could frighten. The process did not, as it often does, confirm a sense of the self as solitary and insolent. On the contrary, he had, through his intellect, discovered his will. He had seen that the only possible dignity would come through meeting his responsibility to other men.

Newport, no longer truly home, was still a place of life and beauty. He renewed his acquaintance with Samuel Hopkins there, attended his widowed mother, spent long days in the Redwood Library. Early in 1802 he returned to Cambridge (and to Tappan) for an A.M. in Theology. In February 1803 he accepted a call from the Federal Street Church and committed himself to the public life of the ministry.

"The sense of duty is the greatest gift of God," Channing later wrote in a discourse called *Honor due to All Men*.[88] His youth had carried him from the assumption of privilege to the consciousness of obligation; he had seen the former squandered and the latter ignored, but he had also seen genuine efforts to act upon old principles in a radically altered world. His adulthood would be an unremitting effort to achieve such a balance of realism and hope.

1

Nature

. . . at last he loses his identity; takes the mystic ocean at his feet
for the visible image of that deep, blue, bottomless soul, pervading
mankind and nature; and every strange, half-seen, gliding, beautiful thing that eludes him; every dimly-discovered, uprising fin of
some undiscernible form, seems to him the embodiment of those
elusive thoughts that only people the soul by continually flitting
through it. In this enchanted mood, thy spirit ebbs away to whence
it came; becomes diffused through time and space; like Cranmer's
sprinkled Pantheistic ashes, forming at last a part of every shore
the round globe over.

There is no life in thee, now, except that rocking life imparted
by a gently rolling ship; by her, borrowed from the sea, from the
inscrutable tides of God. But while this sleep, this dream is on ye,
move your foot or hand an inch; slip your hold at all; and your
identity comes back in horror. Over Descartian vortices you
hover. And perhaps, at midday, in the fairest weather, with one
half-throttled shriek you drop through that transparent air into the
summer sea, no more to rise for ever. Heed it well, ye Pantheists!

—Herman Melville

IN APRIL 1845 Francis Bowen, editor of the *North Ameri-
can Review* and future Alford Professor of Moral Philosophy at
Harvard, published a review of a speculative cosmology that
was eliciting outrage from religious men in England and
America. The book, Robert Chambers's *Vestiges of the Natural
History of Creation*, was published anonymously and would
soon be attributed to a host of secret authors, including Prince
Albert. Proclaiming scandal by its anonymity, it paved the way
for Darwin by drawing off "the first wrath of the critics,"[1] and
Bowen was one of the angriest. He took a condescending tone
toward the work, a quasi-technical narrative about the cooling

of nebulae, solar explosions, and even some speculation that monkeys have a paternal relation to men. It amounts, in Bowen's phrase, to an account of "creation by the natural and unassisted development of the inherent qualities of brute matter." What dampens Bowen's amusement is the temerity of the theory in postulating a universe "without oversight or direction." It is, in short, a blasphemous fantasy of an ungoverned world. This kind of speculation, and Bowen's prickly response, are not remarkable in the pre-Darwin years. The interest lies in the reviewer's sarcasm. His impatience seems a pose: "We need not analyze with any great minuteness the geological facts and hypotheses incorporated into this magnificent history of creation. As will be seen hereafter, the violent and sweeping transformation and convulsions that the earth's crust has undergone directly conflict with our author's theory, and afford the strongest presumption that an extraneous cause has frequently interfered at different periods, to repair the desolation produced by the unassisted working of natural laws."[2] This dismissal of the idea of a universe without moral design rests essentially on two claims: first, that there are signs of supervision (he cites rather skimpy evidence compared to the host of providences once catalogued by New England writers), and second, that the human mind is utterly unequipped to penetrate the question. The first ground is ancient, the second hardly new, but its use by an apostle of reason is more than a little startling. The invocation of human ignorance is a telling irony, one among many that had entrapped Bowen's senior colleague William Ellery Channing, who in 1845 was less than three years dead.

The delight that Francis Bowen takes in pointing out the merely figurative grasp of scientific language not only forecasts the coming split between the literary and scientific minds but is also a plain evasion: his defenses waver at the prospect of a truly thorough demonstration of the triumph of chance in the natural world. His attacks are methodological, almost pedantic. His fear of an idea has resolved into an effort to discredit a method.

Six years earlier Orestes Brownson had suggested, in one historian's paraphrase, that "the charge of skepticism was more clearly applicable to those who could believe nothing without miracles than to those who could believe everything without them."[3] What Brownson had seen was the terrible fragility of the Unitarian cosmos, and at the core of its weakness he saw the failure of nature to stir the rationalist heart. It is a commonplace that the connection that Christian rationalists sought to sustain between reason and revelation was less a fusion than a compromise between those with a mechanical view of nature and those who insisted on the direct communication of the spirit.[4] The achieved balance was precarious, being largely a strategy to supplement the deists and defuse the enthusiasts. But long before 1845 the insistence on what Carlyle would call "natural supernaturalism" became not so much a strategy for dealing with external intellectual threats as a way of coping with internal tension. To the Unitarians, nature on her own was a shaky foundation for faith.[5] They quite literally needed miracles to reassure them of God's active presence in the world—this was the sorry situation at which Emerson expressed incredulity in the *Divinity School Address* (1838). But what Emerson did not point out, and what still needs emphasis, is that the rationalists' uncertainty derived not only, perhaps not even chiefly, from their failure to see the divine energy of nature itself. Bowen, for example, did not shrink from a dead, motionless universe as the residue left by a vanished "oversight and direction"; on the contrary, the world described in the *Vestiges of Natural History* is a pulsating, changing world, very much alive, breathing a life all too much its own. It is much the same world that Darwin would reveal in the tangled bank. And this, not dissipated mechanism, is the real cause of fright. What Bowen tried to dismiss with sarcasm, and what Emerson hardly considered—a world out of control—Channing had already seen.

Channing's statements on nature are usually of the expected kind, those which have earned him his label as an unflappable optimist tired of Calvinist gloom, halfway to the bright romantic morning: "Nature should be studied for its own sake, because so wonderful a work of God, because impressed with his perfection, because radiant with beauty, grandeur, and wisdom, and beneficence." But one soon finds a strange disjunction: such expository praise is rarely matched by heightened descriptive language. There is none of Thoreau's—or Jonathan Edwards's—delight in rolling off natural beauties, no bombardment of images. The receptivity of the human mind is acknowledged; indeed its sensitivity to nature obeys divine decree: "This unbounded creation of sun, and moon, and stars, and clouds, and seasons, was not ordained merely to feed and clothe the body, but first and supremely to awaken, nourish, and expand the soul." And yet this comes near the peak of lyricism in Channing's language, though he reiterates again and again the teleology of nature: "The material organs of sense, especially the eye, wake up infinite thoughts in the mind . . . the universe in which we live, was plainly meant by God to stir [us]." That "faith cometh by hearing," so basic an assumption in the early New England psychology of conversion, is lost to Channing. His recourse to the eye underscores the fallen stature of the sermon. "Preaching," he admits, "is becoming less and less efficacious,"[6] and everywhere latent in his thinking is an envy of those religions that still have the power to spellbind. Infant American Catholicism will pose a special threat.[7] The point here is that though he rejects utilitarian views of nature—so characteristic of eighteenth-century American rationalism[8]—Channing never loses himself fully in the celebration of nature; he will not use her sensually. There is rarely replication, always and only analysis: "[Nature] is full of difficulty and mystery, and can only be penetrated and unravelled . . . Let me strive to convey some precise ideas of [its emotional effect] . . . in doing this, I can use no language which will save the hearer from the necessity of thought . . . I know that these lectures are meant for entertainment rather than mental labor; but as I have told you, I have great faith in labor."[9] The refusal to abandon intellection is adamant.

But the fruits of even the analytic study of nature are not always palatable. "Not a direct or urgent teacher," nature has one great failing: the fact of immortality cannot be learned from her. She was, after all, available to pre-Christian man, and the solace offered by Christ was generous exactly because of nature's failure. Her failure to teach immortality is one thing; a tolerable lapse, it even conforms to the logic of the Unitarian theodicy, since it is a partial evil without which the greater good of Christianity would be redundant. But her active contradiction of the doctrine is quite another thing, deeply troubling, and here Channing's presumed serenity falters. The knowledge of immortality being elusive to the senses, experience of the external world cannot persuade of it. A turn inward is the consequence: "through the soul, much more than through the universe, we arrive at this conception." But the turn is not only from nature's silence, it is also a recoil from her speech. The potential activity of nature frightens more than her passivity frustrates: "A single plant, endued with the principle of unlimited expansion, would in the progress of centuries overshadow nations and exclude every other growth, would exhaust the earth's whole fertility . . . Were the tree to spread indefinitely . . . it would destroy."[10] It is true enough that the subjunctive cast of these ruminations attests that Channing's conception of actual nature is not one of murderous energy. Indeed, natural virtue, here as elsewhere, consists in a principle of self-limitation. But it is crucial to see the movement of his imagination, or rather, its lack of movement: the idea of limitless growth that he assigns to the human mind cannot survive the transfer to the natural world.[11] Though he readily affirms the growth of the mind, the extension of this idea outside the mind yields only images of strangulation.

This obstruction in the imagination of America's leading liberal clergyman is a significant blockage—not a quirk. A regression from the vision of the man whose world view generated the rationalist reaction, it throws into high relief Edwards's joyful assent toward nature. Edwards's delight fills his central treatise, the *Religious Affections* (1746), with metaphor—ratified, not originated, by scripture—casting the regenerate mind as a participant in the organic activity of growth and change: "Grace is compared to a seed implanted, that not only is in the ground, but . . . grows there . . . Godliness in the heart has as direct a relation to practice, as a fountain has to a stream, or as the luminous nature of the sun has to beams sent forth, or as life has to breathing, or the beating of the pulse, or any other vital act."[12] The key word is "vital"; for the stern Calvinist Edwards, similes were simply too weak to show the identity of regenerate man with living nature and with nature's God. For Channing the similes are too strong. Especially as we are accustomed to think of romanticism progressively emerging from the deists, it is worth pausing when the chronology seems reversed. It is doubly fitting to pause because Channing himself exhorts us—and perhaps himself—"to let the spiritual presence of that intensest thinker of the new world [Edwards] . . . stir you up to energy of thought."[13]

One may begin, then, to trace Channing's position by way of negatives: clearly no comfortable deist, he does not retreat from participation into the observer's role. The specter of a clockwork world chills him. "How can one bear," he asks, "to hear Nature called a 'machine'?" And it offends him too, for the laws of uniformity suggest God's preference for "the general good rather than an affection for individuals."[14] This objection would be echoed by his nephew in the 1850s,[15] and it is of course the great imperative answered by the miracles. The insufficiency of nature as moral teacher again manifests divine wisdom: God, like a Boston preacher, speaks more happily with individuals than with the multitude. But the line between explanation and rationalization is thin, and Channing has crossed it. For the obvious question—and it was asked—is, why are the accepted miracles only historical? Why are the reports of thousands of miraculous conversions from Cane Ridge in Kentucky and the burned-over district in New York not admissable to the canon? Why has God ceased to speak to individuals? Acknowledging the question, "Not a few . . . have doubts of the Christian miracles, because they see none *now*," he offers an answer: to bridle at change in God's pedagogical technique is to be "childish," and to deny the idea of progress. He is speaking to the rationalist heart. The fact that in "periods of thick darkness"[16] God did speak dramatically confers no obligation on him to speak so now. Indeed the absence of contemporary miracles attests to human progress. Miracles once proved God's compassion; their obsolescence now proves his adaptability to men's needs. Channing is quite capable of mental gymnastics.

As the deist's universe does not console him, so an animated universe holds perils, if not terrors, for him. The need is for a middle way, and the pastness of the miracles achieves this compromise. It is therefore an indispensable doctrine. And yet Channing assaults it himself: he confesses, and this is a crucial admission, that the disposition to believe in miracles is historically associated with credulity and ignorance. At pains to discredit many miracles, he exempts only those safely embedded in history.[17] The point is not only that the miracles constitute an excruciatingly slender thread by which to maintain connection with divine compassion but also that they test Channing's instincts: he fiercely distrusts the kind of mind that fosters disruption, that celebrates, or worse still instigates, violent change. This is his heritage from Mayhew and Chauncy and even Locke himself, and it is the root of his polemic against the evangelical mind. A miracle is nothing if not an interruption of order. The moment and the purpose must be just right. With the miracles as his only light, Channing must walk very gingerly, for he is taking a path that divides automatism from chaos.

"Animate," then, is a word of varied application for Channing, and the variety means confusion more than delight. The occasion of an address before the Massachusetts Temperance Society "may well animate a Christian minister," but the virtuous must share the word with their enemy: "The lover of social pleasure little dreams, that the glass, which animates conversation, will ever be drunk in solitude." For Channing, not only the context of words but also the context of the human will affects the meaning of an act. In one discourse that sways between the priggish and the comic, he devises a scheme to drain the sex out of dancing. Make it a regular domestic habit, he suggests, and it will lose its glamor and its daring: "Members of the same family, when confined by unfavorable weather, should recur to it for exercise and exhilaration."[18] In Channing's scheme it is not merely the substitution of "innocent pleasures" for destructive ones but rather the relocation from ballroom to livingroom that makes all the difference. This reflects a habit of mind that— when applied to more than dancing—has interesting implications. Certain inclinations in human nature are assumed, and the effort to control them takes the form not of attempted eradication but of altering the configuration in which they exist. This impulse represents in miniature the ideology of reform that filled the American social scene in the decades before the Civil War. "Upon Locke and his psychology," Perry Miller has said, "the Unitarian edifice was constructed."[19] It may be added that upon Locke rested the possibility of ameliorative reform.

Through the sovereignty of environment, the sensationalist psychology held out implicitly an ideal of controlled circumstance that would permit benevolent education.

But already by the turn of the eighteenth century a rash of speculation, notably in English doppelgänger novels by James Hogg, Godwin, and Mary Shelley—all informed by a deep Protestantism[20]—was challenging sensational doctrine. In America, Charles Brockden Brown began to tell dark tales calling into doubt the notion that sin could be starved from without. In many ways the nineteenth century began with a backward leap over the Enlightenment. Channing, born in those critical years, deferred his doubts and joined the voice of New England reason in condemning that leap. It led, after all, not over but into the abyss. The human will required restraints, not stimulants.

To animate, then, is to manipulate, and it is the vainglorious soldier who pre-eminently gives to the idea of manipulation its form. "The military man is the only harlequin left us from ancient times. It is time that his dazzling finery were gone, that it no longer corrupted the young, that it no longer threw a pernicious glare over his terrible vocation."[21] Though Andrew Jackson may have contributed to this composite, the man who more than any other specifies the accusation is Napoleon.

Channing's famous essay on Napoleon is largely an exercise in self-restraint: "Great powers, even in their perversion, attest a glorious nature, and we may feel their grandeur." With typical honesty, Channing claims no immunity from that feeling. It is again a case of impulse misdirected; Napoleon follows immediately after Milton in the collected works whose publication Channing supervised, and since the real subject of the Milton essay is Satan, the proximity is apt. The French, Napoleon's victims, are an "intoxicated people." They have produced faulty institutions—military schools, for example, that inculcate a passivity close to groveling. They have been weakened by a pale national ideology; the "heartless scoffer, Voltaire," has calloused them.[22] Channing was undoubtedly tutored in this animus toward the French by his testy grandfather, who raged at the French occupation during the war years and at their implanting "infidel principles into some of the best minds of Newport."[23] Whatever the source, Channing became convinced that too-long consort with skepticism had starved the French soul and made it long for a taste of the ecstatic. This is one great danger of disrupting the balance that underlies his rationalism. The other equal peril is destroying the balance from the other direction: "Enthusiasts often become skeptics."[24]

But the French are an instance of the first tragedy. Channing, of course, had no monopoly on these worries; the whole Federalist establishment had shuddered at the movement of French society and at the number of its American admirers; thirty years before, the tillers of Timothy Dwight's Greenfield Hill had been called "Back from the wild of guilt and brink of woe/To virtue's house and family,"[25] back from French infidelity to English faith and practice. Indeed after the brief respite of the Adams presidency and some welcome blows to French political prestige like the XYZ Affair, things had only gotten worse: the foreign infidel was becoming domestic in the persons of Jefferson and Madison. The Hartford Convention, where antiwar New England Federalists gathered in 1814 and nearly endorsed secession, could almost seem an opportunity lost to avoid the French contagion and embrace England.

Rushed toward hysteria—a prospectus for what might happen in America—the French are described by Channing in sexual language that is not always covert. He transforms France into an obsequious and emphatically female creature. The vision of sexual outrage is soon eclipsed by the greater outrage of submission: raped, she honors her attacker—"a blood-stained usurper" who "awed and dazzled" her by "conciliating [her] vanity" until she "subjected herself" to him. Even the safer vocabulary of sentimentalism risks suggestive ambiguities: "[Bonaparte] knew that his steps would be followed by the groans of widowed mothers and famished orphans; of bereaved friendship and despairing love."[26] Compare the account by Orville Dewey, one of Channing's eulogists, of a revivalist's work in a New York girls' school: "There were tears and sighs and groans [and] the whole school . . . was convulsed by raptures."[27] Sighs and groans, to the Unitarian mind, were not expressions of the spiritual life. Like Dewey's, Channing's connotation becomes his meaning if compared with Emerson's rather pallid version of Napoleon's appeal: "He filled the troops with his spirit and a sort of freedom and companionship grew up between him and them."[28] To Channing the whole business smells of bestial instinct. A sanguinary coupling of individual and nation, it elicits the ultimate expression of his abhorrence for a society of separate entities collapsed into passionate unity.

The assumptions behind this abhorrence bear importantly on Unitarian Christology, on its banishment of the bleeding Christ, and they have continual reference to Jacksonianism at home. First published in 1827, the Napoleon essay labors to certify the American contrast. At stake is also a domestic contrast, for "slave country reeks with licentiousness," and "licentiousness is fruitful of crime."[29] Even more traversable than the Atlantic, the Mason-Dixon line marks a border of civilization, and the circle of lust and crime must never grow too large to honor the boundary. In such fierce externalization of evil, Channing can be his least honest and his least true to the New England tradition of relentless self-examination. Also an overlooked precedent for such future creations of the New England imagination as Prescott's Cortés and Parkman's Pontiac (figures who repel and excite their chroniclers), the Napoleon essay finally manifests the deepest anxieties of the Unitarian mind. They surface often, if sometimes in less somber, more suspenseful and entertaining ways: "Two or three men, strangers often . . . enter a house . . . with an air of . . . solemnity, and signify their wish to see the family together . . . As the male members of it are commonly absent on their business, they have to deal only with the females of the family. These, with their natural timidity and reserve, sit down in fear and silence, to await the dread communication. Their inquisitors open with the most pointed questions, put in the most awful manner, concerning their most secret, solemn, and delicate feelings . . .''[30] This is Dewey's account, cast in ominous italics, of a *domiciliary visitation* by back-country revivalists; his colleagues, including Channing, would know how to complete the ellipsis.

In their warmer tributes to Napoleon, both Carlyle and Emerson cite the story of the emperor ridiculing a group of atheists by gazing at the sky and saying, "Very good, messieurs, but who made all that?"[31] Their delight in recounting this story is not available to Channing; perhaps neither was the anecdote. But had it been, it would have had no place in his essay, for there can be no hint of piety in his Napoleon. Making the pantheist a hero is unthinkable: "We believe that an enlightened and exalted mind is a brighter manifestation of God, than the outward universe."[32] The studious pantheist may be condemned to disappointment, but the deeper reason that Channing could never embrace the image that Carlyle and Emerson applaud is not a wariness of delusion but rather a horror at the possibility of realization. The wide-open lifeline between nature and man makes monsters, not philosophers. Channing has foreseen and felt the panic at self-immolation that thirty years later would momentarily halt even its most eager celebrant—for even Whitman could be frightened by sensory excitement: "Unclench your floodgates, you are too much for me," he cries in *Song of Myself* to "Blind loving wrestling touch."

"Genius," Channing concurs, "has become a scourge to the world, its breath a poisonous exhalation, its brightness a seducer into paths of pestilence and death." And yet, "it is force . . . in which virtue consists."[33] Many such conflicting pairs could be assembled—the conclusion they press home is that Channing's hesitation before the power of mind is a self-divided one; call it squeamishness or call it conviction, it is a central American predicament in the years before the Civil War.[34] He longs, like his version of the French, for invigoration, and yet he is wary to the depths of his soul of the fanatic. The most fruitful outgrowth of this tension in its capacity to make art will be Melville's Ahab, but all American romanticism will arise from within this opposition.

For English romanticism—as for almost everything English—Channing has praise: "The great poet of our times, Wordsworth . . . has gone to common life . . . to the obscure and neglected portions of society, for beautiful and touching themes." But this is the Wordsworth of *Lyrical Ballads* (1798), speaking still with the sentimentalism of Goldsmith and Crabbe, not the poet of *The Prelude* (1805/50), whom Channing would never know. There is no blurring of nature's autonomy in the Wordsworth Channing knew, no taunting of children, no menacing mountains. Similarly, the terms of praise for Scott select in a way that Wordsworth does not require: "What light has Jeanie Deans shed on the path of the obscure!" Channing is drawn to that heroine, who epitomizes the "cult of benevolence," who can calm a man's rage and pacify a mob. She is the ancestor of Mrs. Gaskell's Margaret Hale and Dickens's Esther Summerson, whom Channing would have commended—as his remarks on Dickens anticipate and the quietism of his essay on Fénelon confirms. These are the relaxed, if not moribund, versions of romanticism that Channing can embrace; though Wordsworth may well be the literary corollary to Napoleon in the guise of the contemplative man, Channing accepts him. What he cannot accept is that "the most stirring is the most popular poetry, even though it issue from the desolate soul of a misanthrope and libertine."[35] Byron goes too far.

Natural and savage, then, if not synonymous descriptives, are finally distinguished in Channing's mind by degrees. The terror of Napoleon—and it is truly an existential terror for the very reason that he is so attractive, so seductive—is his brilliant enactment of natural force; he is the Darwinian survivor exemplified. When an idea has not yet been granted a name—as cutthroat nature had not in 1827—when it is without disarming jargon, when intuition knows it better than the analytical faculties of mind, then it is most threatening. This is the meaning of Napoleon for Channing.

"Hitherto it has been assumed that all our knowledge must conform to objects. But all attempts to ascertain anything about them *a priori* by concepts, and thus to extend our knowledge, came to nothing on this assumption. Let us try, then, whether we may not make better progress in the tasks of metaphysics if we assume that objects must conform to our knowledge."[36] Channing probably never read this gentle announcement of Kant's "Copernican revolution." Unlike Francis Bowen, he did not roll up his sleeves and fight the good fight against German subversion, but through the fellowship of literate New Englanders like Charles Follen, the appreciative pages of Mme de Staël, and possibly Coleridge's *Aids to Reflection* (1825), he absorbed at least some of the impact of German thought.[37] He shows, moreover, an explicit awareness of the epistemological dead end to which Hume had led the Western mind, and his response is especially revealing.[38] Partly a return to comforting old ground, it is also a tentative move toward a position not unlike the transcendental one; this simultaneous retreat and advance expresses something of the depth of his dilemma.

Hume, to put it crudely, had stretched the distance between man and nature into a gulf. Channing certainly did not tackle the problem of causality in its full complexity—as indeed probably no American since Edwards had been equipped to do—but he felt the crisis and passionately averred the intelligibility of events. "All the evidences of Christianity," he preached in 1821, "may be traced to this great principle—that every effect must have an adequate cause." While the orthodox shuddered, Channing all but admitted that another name for Christianity, a name for faith, is the principle of causality. Reduced to helpless spectating on the world, he looks for a way to enter it again: "God's infinity has its image in the soul . . . I have no fear of expressing too strongly the connection between the Divine and the human mind." It is this insistence on symmetry between man and God that blunts for Channing the skeptic's attack: "A necessary part or principle of our mental constitution . . . is . . . the disposition to trace effects to adequate causes. We are indeed so framed, as to expect a continuance of that order."[39] Enlisting Scottish common sense against Scottish skepticism, it is hardly a resounding answer, but it is Channing's faith.[40] It is also one of those moments when he foreshadows the pragmatism that would become a distinctively American philosophy: he simply must trust the apprehensions of his mind. Not far from the classical idea of man as microcosm, Channing's is a static vision of the mind as mirror to divinity much more than it is a Kantian idea of internal concepts giving form to apprehended phenomena. And yet, from a position that implies utter separation of subject and object—the position represented by Hume—he is attempting to grasp a notion of active participation by the mind in the apprehension of reality. He has not returned to innate ideas, but he is seeking a kind of intuitive consciousness to which objects and events conform.

He will not explore the "reality" of the intuited forms, nor ponder the relation of apprehended appearance to things-in-themselves, nor wonder whether things-in-themselves are knowable. He bears no intellectual comparison whatever with Kant, and yet he is sensitive to the same fatigue in the tradition of rationalism that inspired the great critical revolt. Immortality, that most crucial of Kant's postulates for rendering possible the moral life, is for Channing as well an extraphenomenal truth. He turns inward with none of the systematic fury that fires the first *Critique*, and yet he does turn, instinctively finding experience an insufficient teacher. It is a poignant reminder of the unity of human concern to watch Channing in the New World—whose provincialism so unnerved him—as he begins to feel the same restiveness, the same stirrings, that, through a professor in Königsberg, would change the direction of Western thought.

In dealing with Channing's generation and the Transcendentalists who followed, the question is not whether they understood what Kant meant, but what they understood him to mean. By conceding the inadequacy of reason to know God, Kant may have liberated faith for Theodore Parker, but to Orestes Brownson he had mortally wounded it. To Andrews Norton it was all a wild blaspheming.[41] To a rational Unitarian, the separation of reason from religion—even if it retained a "regulative" role— was a disaster. As the miracle controversy preeminently shows, the senses and conscious rational faculties had to participate in the growth of religious conviction. The Unitarian concept of conversion, if it can be called such, is a building-block theory, and some of the crucial blocks are removed by the transcendental argument.[42] The central point for understanding Channing is that he is finally not unwilling—in spite of all his instinctive reluctance—to alter the bond between man and nature in the direction of identity; he is willing to seek truth in the mental process itself (this is his embryonic pragmatism). In all this, he elicits shudders not only from the orthodox but from his more conservative colleagues, for as Kant and Cousin and Schelling began arriving in America in various states of misrepresentation, most Unitarians panicked.[43]

The reception of the "idealist" philosophers is itself potent testimony to the subjectivity of human perception, since the response invariably tells more about receiver than received.

That Channing did not recoil in horror is the surest sign of his hunger for a psychology beyond Locke, though he clings to miracles as God's recognition of the senses as conduit to the soul. He hungers for a world view beyond Shaftesbury, though he prefers static nature to an expanding one; and for an epistemology beyond Reid, though he cherishes common sense. That he does not flee to Locke, or, like Francis Bowen, into the arms of Bishop Berkeley, is telling. Bowen, whose sensitivities are again reliable signals of vulnerable spots in the rationalist world view, embraces Berkeley as if he were a prodigal ally returned to the fold. To witness this reunion is to see rationalism in full flight, a defensive condition from which Channing feels more and more estranged. Berkeley is ultimately comforting to Bowen because he separates man from nature and interposes God. The line has been cut between the human mind and anything beyond phenomena—a situation that can carry a terrible charge of loneliness. But to Bowen, with enthusiasts and ranters foremost on his mind, the overwhelming impact is an enforced humility for those who would know too much: "it is the part of overweening self-confidence to suppose that the problem is altogether insoluble because *we* cannot find an answer to it; that the ocean is boundless because *our* lines cannot fathom it."[44] A condescending chuckle sounds through these words; one suspects that Bowen's patrician self-image escapes the indictment carried by the first-person pronouns. But whether or not he spares himself, the key point is his satisfaction at what he considers a stop to man's attrition of God's prerogatives. All coherence, in the Berkeleyan world, comes through the grace of God. In retreat the Unitarian has found a belated substitute for the divine omnipotence against which he had once advanced.

This achieved distance between nature and man, with the inscrutable deity intervened, is inadequate for Channing, who can praise the Bishop only guardedly.[45] Though it does answer his need for a restraint in the intimacy of man with nature, it answers it too radically. For finally, Channing is the greater humanist, and perhaps paradoxically, it is his advocacy of man that withholds from his language the poetry that worship can release. Bowen, by contrast, can speak real beauty, even echoing the "Augustinian strain of piety" that flowed through an earlier New England. He celebrates an ongoing intimacy between creator and creation, a sentient relation such that every motion wrought by God is felt by him as an insult to his person. The image holds no touch of lewdness, as it is not so much the relation of two bodies as that of a soul to its own body: "Is it irreverent, then, to suppose that this union of body and soul shadows forth the connection between the material universe and the infinite one? . . . The unity of action, the regularity of antecedence and the consequence in outward events, which we commonly designate by the lame metaphor of *law*, then become the fitting expression of the consistent doings of an all-wise Being, in whom there is no variableness, neither shadow of turning. The Creator, then, is no longer banished from his Creation, nor is the latter an orphan, or a deserted child."[46] God wears his universe like a garment. This vision is not beyond, or beneath, but outside the sensibility of Channing. For him, such a union is too private; man cannot be so totally excluded from the life of the cosmos even as a rescued child, and this is why he drifts from colleagues like Bowen; this is why he moves carefully but steadily toward the consolidated vision of the romantics. What makes him so human is his profound uncertainty along the way. And it is this willingness, this flexibility of mind, that eventually forces him to confront the Napoleonic monster in all its manifestations: in Andrew Jackson, in Charles Grandison Finney, in the foaming abolitionists. The allowance of divine attributes to man may avert epistemological chaos, but it may also license the ancient passion of Antichrist: pride.

Frailty and early death among the liberal clergy have often

been remarked.[47] Although he lived into his sixties, Channing was, or considered himself, sickly all his life. How much this bears on his wariness of high natural force—whether as cause or consequence—is a question to be returned to. One more danger, however, afflicts Channing's qualified assent to nature and the participating mind. Perhaps as difficult to resolve as the question of his health, it is potentially more serious.

Channing claims to fear "that insane, desperate unbelief which strives to quench the light of nature as well as of revelation, and to leave us not only without Christ, but without God . . . no more than . . . the efforts of men to pluck the sun from his sphere, or to storm the skies with the artillery of the earth." The impression is inescapable that he protests too much. There is strain—debilitating strain—implicit in his vacillation and uncertainty. To tap the demonic, no matter how slightly, is a perilous therapy, and this, in the end, is what Channing has done. To say that his tentative steps toward deifying man are a shoring up of failing faith is to put it too strongly, but to deny the vulnerability of that faith is to make a worse distortion. By temperament, Channing abhors the mob mentality, "getting warm in crowds"; he detests the demagogue and shrinks from unchecked passion. "Society is now a quick-shifting pageant," he said five years before his death, "[with] the former stability of things . . . strikingly impaired." The wake of the French Revolution still carries "scenes . . . shocking to the calm and searching eye of reason," and yet "the world . . . is more than ever penetrated with the spirit of humanity" and "we live under brighter lights than former generations." The sheer energy of nature—toward which Channing shows such deep ambivalence —has been infused into history, and thus into the agents of history: the minds of men. "The mind is awakening to a consciousness of what it is, and of what it is made for."[48] What is so remarkable in view of his inheritance, indeed of his very being, is that Channing ultimately assents to this infusion. It is a hard thing for such a man to leave the decorous precincts of reason. But he takes the step.

Much has been overcome, but great obstacles remain. This, again, is his most stringent collar: "Enthusiasts often become skeptics." The darkest insight for Channing, it pursues him in his search for renewal, it informs his vision of the possibilities of spiritual rebirth, and more than anything it can lend a flavor of fantastic resignation to his confession: "I believe Christianity to be true, or to have come from God, because it seems to me impossible to trace it to any other origin."[49] It is faith by a process of elimination. So much of Channing's work constitutes a dismantling of nature and a discrediting of history: this is the precious residue.

"We must see and feel the broad distance between the spiritual life within us, and the vegetable or animal life which acts around us."[50] It is crucial for an understanding of Channing, and germane to all American liberalism, to see that this turn toward man is intimately connected to, indeed is the selfsame act as, the turn away from nature. There is, moreover, a hortatory tone in Channing's "we must feel." His credo rarely resounds, it is always bittersweet. Perhaps this wistfulness is what Sydney Ahlstrom had in mind when he called attention to the strange urgency—beyond the power of his prose, or the originality of his mind—with which Channing touched the heart of his age.[51]

However embryonic, the romantic inversion of dependency of mind on object could generate a vertigo that Channing's generation recognized as their special dilemma. For they faced the specter of a chameleon universe, one that torments its rational inhabitants by catering too personally to the whims of individuals, shutting off man from man. This is the prospect that Edwards had forestalled by documenting God's vocabulary in the notebook which Perry Miller called *Images or Shadows of Divine Things*; the prospect that sent Bowen back to Berkeley. Emerson, too, would feel the problem of communication between eternally isolated selves, each communicating with the over-soul through his own secreted forms, and so would Hawthorne: "If thou hadst a sorrow of thine own, the brook might tell thee of it . . . even as it is telling me of mine."[52] Channing, uneasy in his Federal Street pulpit, remains more worried that the world might fall silent than that it might erupt into cacophony.

There runs through the mid-century American mind a deep and shared concern that the Kantians have triggered a hypertrophy of the self. "We cannot understand," says Brownson in his review of the *Divinity School Address*, "how it is possible for a man to become virtuous by yielding to his instincts." The stuffier Francis Bowen relies more for a counterweapon on the limits of the human mind: "The imperfection of our faculties lies at the bottom . . . Human ingenuity can weave puzzles, which human intellect cannot solve."[53] These and many other such retreats from the religion of the self constitute a very important dissent—of which Channing is both target and participant. For him this stream of caution sometimes widens into fear, and it is a soul-deep feeling, for, as we shall see, the self becomes more and more his sanctuary as, one by one, nature, history, and scripture drop away.

"There is always an appeal open from criticism to nature," said the great classic voice of eighteenth-century England,[54] and indeed a reductionist account might call Channing's sensibility broadly classical; he does share Johnson's distaste for the "promiscuous" celebration of nature. And yet the label fits badly, since for Johnson the appeal remained open while for Channing it threatened to close. In America nature was darkening. By midcentury her novelists would write more of lust and carnage than of the picturesque, and Channing saw the beginnings of this descent. Without laboring or exaggerating, he cannot be construed as progenitor of major intellectual lines. He did not lend himself to proselytizing, and his very essence—his sensitivity to half-truths and awareness of dualities—threatened to preclude engagement to a cause. He has affinities: with Emerson, with William James. But he has no school. The source of his pathos— what makes him compelling—may finally be his suspicion, perhaps unconscious, that the habitual forms of soft-spoken piety concealed rationalizations for the invisibility of God: "One of the mysteries of the universe is this, that its Author retires so continually behind the veil of his works, that the . . . Father does not manifest himself more distinctly to his creatures." But Channing shuts off his yearning when it begins to rise into protest: "The electric fluid, unseen, unfelt, and everywhere diffused, is infinitely more efficient, and ministers to infinitely nobler productions, than when it breaks forth in thunder."[55] Everything that he held precious combined to ratify this proscription, and yet he needed—notwithstanding his lifelong disclaimer—to hear more thunder.

2
The
Flight
from
History

All that a historian won was a vehement wish to escape . . . As a matter of taste, he greatly preferred his eighteenth-century education when God was a father and nature a mother, and all was for the best in a scientific universe. He repudiated all share in the world as it was to be, and yet he could not detect the point where his responsibility began or ended.

—Henry Adams

STUDENTS OF American literature are often introduced to nineteenth-century liberal religion through a pleasant story. First told by Channing himself, since repeated by generations of lecturers, it tells of the young Channing's attendance with his father at a sermon by a popular revival preacher in the neighborhood of Newport. This minister, by Channing's account, delivered a scalding imprecation in the grand hellfire tradition, and the boy quaked. Silent in its aftermath, he sat with his father during the carriage ride home, watching him, we might suppose, light his pipe and hearing him pronounce, between puffs, "sound doctrine, fine sermon." A Sunday feast probably followed, then a lazy afternoon devoted to digestion. And so, Channing's account concludes, the future minister had learned that the doctrines of depravity and damnation could not be true; if they were, no one could have such composure.[1]

The weight of this occasion may fall more on the question of the father's sincerity than on that of the preacher's veracity, but it is enough to note that the boy was shaken; the experience remained with him. In 1836 he remembered the man he most closely associated with the old "Calvinism"—Samuel Hopkins—who, if not the preacher in this tale, was the source of an ongoing challenge to Newport's complacence, and whose sermons might well have coalesced into this recollection of a single Sunday. Channing remembered him, or chose publicly to characterize him, as a good and burdened man with a distaste for the things of this world: "He took refuge," Channing recalls, "from the present state of things in the Millennium."[2] Cushioned by respect for Hopkins's integrity, the judgment is implicitly negative. But before calling Hopkins otherworldly or isolated from his worldly congregation, one must recall, as Channing did, that the Newport gentlemen filled the coffers of the First Congregational with rum money, to put it politely, or, more crudely, with the sweat and blood of slaves—and that Hopkins, without flinching, preached abolition to their faces.[3] Channing could never quite come to terms with such emphatically political use of the pulpit. The distinction between affront and crusade would continue to elude him; its pursuit would underlie his lifelong ambivalence toward the abolitionist movement. Indeed the special moral authority of Hopkins needs to be acknowledged in order to see the emotional charge in Channing's refutation of his eschatology: the dismissal may be self-protective. For Channing himself, more than Hopkins, turns with increasing urgency away from history and seeks his own kind of refuge.

That nature and history might be moving together toward a common catastrophe was for Channing a real possibility, and by the 1830s it was becoming a reality. The times were "hurried, bustling, tumultuous," the age "selfish, mercenary, sensual."[4] Essentially, the fears of the Napoleon essay have been realized, but with the difference that the unwelcome natural force has not cohered in America—though it once threatened to, it has not welded a man to a nation. By the late thirties Channing is concerned less with enslavement of the popular will than with general incoherence. It is in this period that he becomes so sensitive to the feigning, the prevarication, the layers of posing that attend every utterance in the slavery debate. America has become a collection of self-interested combatants, swirling about one another. Nature's cardinal failure is history's too. The individual means nothing to the tide, which, once released, is relentless: "Ages may not see the catastrophe of the tragedy, the first scene of which we are so ready to enact; [the annexation of Texas] will be linked by an iron necessity to long-continued deeds of rapine and blood."[5] One year later Nathaniel Hawthorne, in high expression of what Melville called his "Calvinistic sense of Innate Depravity and Original Sin," would "exemplify how an influence beyond our control lays its strong hand on every deed which we do, and weaves its consequences into an iron tissue of necessity."[6] Hawthorne's and Channing's phrases reveal a fundamental inclination of the New England mind, its sense of "fate . . . turning on the pivot,"[7] of a critical moment in which the future is born. Hawthorne writes of the manifest destiny of individuals, in this case of a man driven by a fierce desire to spy, disguised, upon his home, his friends, his family. Channing's is a horrified acquiescence to the manifest destiny of nations, leaving only one course open: to escape the chain of consequence he must look to the very sanctuary that Hawthorne finds suffocating, the individual consciousness. And when Channing tries to protect that sanctuary, as he will rather desperately, he will flounder in the bottomless self and feel the fatigue, ultimately the same loneliness that tempts Clifford Pyncheon at his Salem window. In retreating inward from history—

as from nature—Channing will feel a ceaseless pressure from the external imperatives of social existence; his reclusive individual will be pressed and twisted and finally misshapen.

One way of describing the process of his retreat is to say that the imagination that failed before restless nature—the unchecked tree—is failing before America herself. Channing cannot construe the nation's expansion as anything other than cancerous: America, he urges Henry Clay, must place "an immediate curb on its passion for extended territory . . . We boast of our rapid growth, forgetting that . . . noble growths are slow. Our people throw themselves beyond the bounds of civilization, and expose themselves to relapses into a semi-barbarous state." To Channing's horror, America is indeed "nature's nation"; he has learned the Turner Thesis, which would proclaim the frontier as the shaper of American destiny, before he could know its name, and thinks it terribly right. Indeed "the frank spirit of the West"—using "frank" to mean hostile as it still does in diplomats' communiqués—is not restricted to the new territories. The frankness seeps eastward: "A witty foreigner observed of the city of Washington, that it had one merit, if no other; it was a city of 'magnificent distances.' For this kind of magnificence our people have a decided taste." The condescension of the foreigner and of the Federal Street preacher are hardly divided by the quotation marks. Of course Washington is not Boston, but the Brahmin's self-control, his contemplative virtues, are also becoming anachronistic in a country "distinguished by . . . premature growth," where "young men come forward sooner into life," and "the mind . . . is exhausted by excess of action."[8]

If American rationalists of the previous century were nervous in their wilderness, more than one "witty foreigner" methodically made matters worse. Thomas Jefferson, for example, wrote his *Notes on Virginia* (1787) largely to answer such a foreigner. The French naturalist Buffon had noted the hairlessness of scrawny Indians, measured their sexual urge and organs, and concluded that the New World stunts, weakens, and generally subjects human beings to decay. "The savage . . . has no hair, no beard, no ardour for the female . . . In this new world . . . there must be something in the combination of the elements . . .which opposes the aggrandisement of animated nature; there must be obstacles to the . . . principles of life."[9] To deny similar French slander, Charles Brockden Brown would later write a series of dissenting footnotes to Volney's *View of the Soil and Climate of the United States* (1804); in neither case are defensiveness and indignation entirely distinct. But by the third decade of the nineteenth century the contemplation of American nature was yielding somewhat different anxieties. Savagery, more than impotence, seemed to be its gift. Bloodthirst becomes a common condition in the early novel, in the romance, and in historical writing: Robert Bird's Nathan Slaughter insanely etches the chests of his victims; Brown's Edgar Huntly "laved [his] head, neck, and arms" in the blood of his first Indian; Prescott (whose life Brown wrote for Jared Sparks's *American Biography*) makes his hero Cortés devour a bloody horse "even to his hide," thus blurring the line between the hero and his Aztec enemies. Even at midcentury, Thoreau taunts his readers by confessing his desire to gobble a woodchuck alive, and Poe's Arthur Pym takes a tentative step toward a piece of human flesh dropped by a sated seagull.[10] In Melville, the attribution of savage nature to man will leave the level of sensationalism and reach for the tragic.

Channing, then, is hardly alone with his ambivalence, and with his sense that "rapine and blood" will rise inevitably from the American continent. His anxieties are characteristic already of the 1820s; indeed his retreat before acceleration bears its closest parallel to Washington Irving, almost an exact contemporary. Consider Irving's meditation on death in *The Sketch Book* (1820): Without death, "the fecundity of nature would be a grievance instead of a blessing. The earth would groan with rank and excessive vegetation, and its surface become a tangled wilderness." Very explicitly, America threatens rankness. Irving's recourse, like Channing's, is always to England. In an act of self-defense, his imagination recasts the flowing Hudson in the image of a "glassy" English lake. The river, currentless, lies "far, far below him . . . [with] a lagging bark here and there sleeping on its glassy bosom."[11] For Channing, who never consciously wrote fictional prose, the key to the contrast that Irving disguises (and thus implicitly admits) lies finally in history. And this is where Channing both anticipates and moves beyond the embryonic horror tales of the young American literary imagination—to something that foreshadows the cosmic pessimism of later generations.

For Channing finds the roots of chaos in the genesis and being of America itself. "We owe this [restless, wild] spirit, in a measure, to our descent from men who left the old world for the new, the seats of ancient civilization for a wilderness."[12] Where George Bancroft would celebrate the providential migration and Francis Parkman would find "vigor," "sinews," and "strong good sense,"[13] Channing finds the seeds of barbarism. To understand this difference between New Englanders of roughly equivalent caste would require multiple biography, but it is possible at least to demonstrate that Channing's frank unease with American origins is far more than a belated rebellion against Puritans, far more than a petty adjunct to the moral argument against Calvinism. It is more because it eradicates the sanctuary of the past, again insuring the individual consciousness as last resort, and signaling a characteristic dilemma of the age. The more recent past, too, is a hard house to reenter. Already a phantom place, it is knowable only through what emerges from it—and when Channing explores it, he loses sight, within a sentence, of the object of his search: "What, I ask, are the proofs of the American revolution? Have we none but written or oral testimony? Our free constitution, the whole form of our society, the language and spirit of our laws, all these bear witness to our English origin, and to our successful conflict for independence."[14] The break with England, which begins as the object of the question, ends as an afterthought. Some historical moments, more recent than the seventeeth-century migration, have lost their consolatory force. One more foundation for intellectual security is shaken here: nature herself has failed as recourse, and nature's sometime ally, history, is failing too. If Channing denied himself the refuge that Hopkins sought in the millennial future, he has also denied himself that other orthodox comfort, refuge in history. He is stuck, self-consciously and unhappily, with the present.

The discrediting of the American past—distant and recent—in Channing's mind, as in the mind of his time, is a complex and painful process. As the idea of history more and more became synonymous with the working out of nature in America, its failure inevitably became the failure of home. Of course the self-flattery in New England's idea of its own historical centrality did not await Channing as its first debunker, nor end with him. From Gershom Bulkeley in *Will and Doom* (1692) to Henry James, who would lampoon Edwards in *Roderick Hudson* (1876) for the nonsense of centering the spiritual world in Northampton, assaults upon the idea are usually associated with minds unhappy with American provincialism—and Channing is no exception. But it is necessary to remember that there are other mind-sets that can oppose the idea of New England's special errand. As one historian has pointed out, Edwards himself could "exorcise from his thinking all thoughts whatever of a special New England history"[15] in order to preserve his vision of universal redemption. The irony is that Channing, well into the age of "scientific history," did retain a sense of American specialness; but it was less providential than aberrant.

His ambivalence toward home was never simplified into

secure Anglophilia. Indeed there was precious little psychological security in American Toryism or its legacy. The hallmark is unsettledness; the dogmatic certainty of a Fisher Ames is rare. The condition of undefined selfhood tested those who could relish the aimlessness, or worse still, the earnestness of their country's youth. Consequently, the literature of the early republic is an anthology of devices for self-persuasion. Even such a patriotic propaganda poem as John Trumbull's *M'Fingal* (1776), which Channing probably read at Harvard, is a bundle of hesitations. Written consciously in the tradition of Milton and Dryden, its portrait of a tempter offers a loyalist oaf whose most sophisticated argument credits Laud with the founding of New England; the impression is inescapable that Trumbull is leery of formulating strong Tory arguments for fear that he might be convinced by his own constructs. This is the limbo that in one form or another distresses so many rational intellectuals of the nation's early years. It is at work in Benjamin Franklin's frantic assertion of independence from his father, from his older brother, and from England—all while he tries to establish a mini-Royal Society in Philadelphia. It is indeed a limbo built into the very conventions through which American writers worked: Royall Tyler's early polemic against English ways, *The Contrast* (1787), simply cannot escape its derivativeness, since every exchange of dialogue smacks of Sheridan. Fenimore Cooper, the story goes, turned to writing when his wife sang the virtues of Austen's *Persuasion*: "I can do better," Cooper insisted—the result was *Precaution* (1820), fortunately his last exercise in the Austen mode. Even fifty years after the Revolution, when much of this psychodrama had run its course, Channing could still introduce Andrews Norton to an English host as "one of the few among us to whom [the] name [of scholar] would be given in your country."[16] The complex persists. Such wide and deep insecurity before English models cannot be completely recounted through institutional or even cultural history. To the men who lived it, it penetrated to the inner life. For one caught in its crest, the colonial governor of Massachusetts, Thomas Hutchinson, it has recently been narrated as an "ordeal," the ordeal of a man who loved America but could imagine it only as a mirror of England. For Channing, who was twenty when Hutchinson died, the feeling may have been less sudden and less humiliating, but its long reign still sapped and saddened him. And its debilitating force was augmented as England herself offered less and less of a liferaft. When American history seems merely aberrant it may be somehow accounted for, but when the mainstream from which America has wandered seems also to forsake its proper path, then prospects more deeply darken. "Who can fathom the depths of guilt and woe in that rich, prosperous island? Is there another spot on earth, in which so many crimes and agonies are accumulated, as in London?"[17] These questions, which Channing posed in 1839, had been unutterable a decade before.

Approaching sixty, increasingly at sea, Channing feels a notable fatigue. "He who retires from active pursuits is as little known to the rising generation as if he were dead . . . New actors hurry the old ones from the stage."[18] Brahmin Boston cannot escape the tide, and the poignancy of Channing's late years is audible here; these are the words of a man lost in his own house—not a pleasant spectacle. Though this experience is hardly confined to his historical moment, it is the special bewilderment of his generation. Never exactly young Turks, the New England intellectuals for whom Channing speaks were born too late to feel the revolution except through the queasiness of their fathers, even a little too late to funnel their energies into Federalist indignation. To Channing's insecurity before nature there is added an unease with history and home. Its literary consequence is an adumbration of the lyrical despair that would fully emerge only with high Victorianism. Channing expresses, in prose, the exhausting insomnia that Tennyson and Swinburne would turn to verse in such poems as *Tithonus* (1842) and *Laus Veneris* (1866): "Sleep is a function of our present animal frame, and let not the transgressor anticipate this boon in the world of retribution before him. It may be, and he has reason to fear, that in that state repose will not weight down his eyelids, that conscience will not slumber there, that night and day the same approaching voice is to cry within, that unrepented sin will fasten with unrelaxing grasp on the ever-waking soul."[19] Only because this is internalized torture rather than brimstone might it horrify a child less than did hellfire in Newport. Amalgamating Puritan imprecation and Victorian anxiety, Channing feels one behind him, the other before him. Neither time past nor future time promises comfort.

Recent work by David Hackett Fischer has suggested that the early decades of the nineteenth century saw the beginning of the end of veneration for age in American society,[20] and the literature of the postrevolutionary years tends to support this thesis: only consider the amnesia and abuse of Rip Van Winkle, or the harassment and exile of Natty Bumppo. It may be that such imaginings conceal the self-indulgence of those who would prefer that the portraits in local taverns still depicted George III rather than George Washington; it may also be that the impudence attributed to the young was a nasty name for nationalism. But in any case, Channing's vision of hell as eternal wakefulness—with its implication that much of life's sweetness rests in its possibilities for slumber—may be allowed to stand for the discontent of a tired generation.

Channing's may be a self-inflicted melancholy, but it is not one that he secretly savors, nor is it deviant. It participates in the mental life of his peers but is not reducible to a social symptom. In a provocative chapter of her study of nineteenth-century New England, Ann Douglas has shown how the liberal mind turned from time, suspending exemplary biography in thick sentimentality, eradicating dates, blurring historical context, filling its biographies instead with "organic markers—birth, conversion, marriage, aging, and above all, illness and death," thus rendering "biography . . . something close to a vegetation myth." Channing too makes this reversion into an ahistorical present, but he cannot be comfortable with it—he cannot, by ignoring the past, rid himself of its weight. His is not so much "a curious immunity to history," as a strenuous effort to find an alternative upon which to base his selfhood and that of his nation.[21] Indeed this discomfort furnishes another clue to his contemporary prestige. It may be that Channing stirred the inquiring and critical instinct in a way that his colleagues did not because he would not quite surrender the integrity of the examined life, because he would not rest with the conventions of historical disregard and nascent solipsism that were enfeebling the New England mind. The turn from history carries a double shame, and Channing feels both charges: it smacks of timidity in the face of what is real, and it threatens to deprive the human spirit of what Channing avers to be the only guarantor of human dignity, time.

For time is the only dimension through which a being may fulfill himself; his humanity lives through his growth, through his ability to respond with some measure of self-consciousness to experience. Jonathan Edwards, seventy years before Channing's maturity, had defended the imputation of original sin on the ground that man—unique among creatures—shares in the identity of his fellow men, both dead and unborn.[22] Indeed American Protestantism had long insisted that a man not only can call upon his personal past in facing new experience but can participate—must participate—in the collective history of humanity. Time, for Edwards, confirmed both man's depravity and his brotherhood. And though Channing fights a continuing battle against the first doctrine (perhaps believing it more than he admits), he also requires history to support the second (perhaps feeling it less than he claims).

Time is indispensable, and yet it is a torturer. Tantalizing, it plays reversals, making yesterday's safe assumption today's error: "The means of keeping order in one state of society, may become the chief excitement of discontent and disorder in another." Of what value is tradition in a world where the strongest advocates of "the argument from duration"[23] are the apologists for slavery? This historicist view of social function is one of the many elements in Channing's thought that undercut the stability of truth (another crucial point at which he diverges from the classical); indeed it is time itself that enforces a utilitarian theory of value. Once useful for control, the old-world aristocracy now feeds agitation. At cruxes like this Channing moves perilously close to moral relativism, a danger to which he is sensitive. The ephemeral nature of cultural assumptions becomes evident to him. With his lifelong deference to the old world, he looks to Europe in 1840 and sees a new specter: potential immigrants, waves of them; "many among us . . . will be more and more infected." What was once instruction has become infection. Channing's dismay may be taken as he offers it, as a concern for American labor thrown into competition "against the half-famished, ignorant workmen of Europe, who will toil for any wages,"[24] or it may be taken as another expression of his fear of social disorder, or as a mixture of both. In any case the ironies of time remain in force. Nothing can be judged any more according to precedent. Once the source of manners, Europe is now an overflowing cesspool: as if she has been transformed by sudden legerdemain from a beauty into a hag, Channing stands before her dumbfounded and a little ridiculous. Yet he recovers enough to give this succinct warning: "Nothing decides the character of a people more than the form and determination of labor."[25] Even when celebrated in almost

Whitmanesque terms, Channing's laborer remains essentially a fitter-in. If his heroism lies in his willingness to dream the American dream of social mobility, it also divests him of all threatening character and reinforces Channing's conviction that near the heart of the evil of slavery is its placing of a man in a position where social malice becomes inevitable; it instigates bitterness where the Northern system, at worst, produces controlled ambition. This is a pre-emptive denial of George Fitzhugh, who would argue in the 1850s that industry made men more miserable and more savage than chattel slavery could ever do.

Even more characteristic are Channing's appeals under stress to a species whose extinction, or at least subordination, is evident in the new society. He posits "an enlightened farmer, who understands agricultural laws of chemistry . . . [and] the properties of manures,"[26] as the model to which "the unthinking peasant" should aspire. Indeed his imagined audience conforms best to the Jeffersonian gentleman—an ideal he witnessed more in his Richmond days than in Newport, and one already fragile at the turn of the century. The pastoral actors whom he directs are obsolete if not already mythic, and he makes little mention of the obstacles that self-culture will encounter in Boston shoe factories and Lowell mills.

Channing's awareness of the pace of social change, then, is variable; sometimes acute, as in his sensitivity to America's shift from colony to colonialist, it is more often naive: "I have seen a distinguished chemist covered with dust like a laborer. Still [he was] not degraded." In 1838 he can still absolve the dust on the scientist's clothing and think he has thereby neutralized that which corrodes the laborer's dignity. Sometimes Channing is neither acute nor naive, but self-deceiving, as in listing the anachronistic follies of Catholicism, a catalogue offered during a lecture that shivers at the raw power of Catholic appeal on the Western frontier.[27] Nothing is stable anymore. An escape into historical "immunity" is sweetly tempting.

But to freeze time is to embrace stagnation. It is to deny progress as well as decay, to weaken the will of men to make a moral investment in the human future. A sense of history is necessary for a sense of destiny. Possessing both and alarmed by both, Channing will not relinquish either: "To suppose no connexion to exist between the present and future character is to take away the use of the present state."[28] It is to call the world gibberish, to acquiesce in cynicism, even nihilism. To freeze time, then, is unthinkable; but time may, with delicacy and caution, be expropriated from the mass and transferred to the individual, in whose care it can be slowed and contained and made less dizzying. Just as he would take the sex out of dancing and the restlessness out of workers, Channing would, in truly puritan dissent, replace the theater with recitation. Bring it out of the crowd and into the drawing-room. Though not "radically evil," the theater nevertheless sports "exhibitions of dancing fit only for brothels," but "a work of genius," he tells us, "recited by a man of fine taste, enthusiasm, and powers of elocution, is a very pure and high gratification."[29] For a man who calls the doctrine of depravity absurd, Channing is strangely eager to keep the human creature where its impulses can be safely channeled, essentially alone. As in the quarrel with dancing, it is necessary to look beyond the banality of the particular remedy to the general principle suggested by the problem. Channing champions domestic recitation for the same reason that he defends poetry in the New World, for what he really admires so much in Milton is his capacity to turn Satan to poetic use, to harness him. This gift for tapping, and controlling, the deepest human energies lies near the heart of Channing's idea of genius. The triumph of this twin achievement may come home to us if we consider that Channing's age had to contend with the internalization of time that Kantian idealism had fostered. The idea of objective time would never quite recover. The greatest American chronicler would once again be Melville, who would allow the white whale to render tidal charts absurdly obsolete by surfacing in Atlantic and Pacific waters simultaneously. Time, then, is becoming a treacherous foundation—another subjective force—and Channing's tactic is to allow it free reign, indeed to praise and sanctify it, within the individual, in the hope that that is where it will stay. This balance between mindless antihistory and assent to change is what finally distinguishes him from the faint-hearted biographers whom Ann Douglas attacks. Channing feels, with a constant gnawing, the tenuousness of his compromise.

The compromise manifests itself most clearly in his doctrines of reform, especially in the lectures on "elevation" of the laboring classes. These lectures, published in 1840, give the fullest expression of his prescription for "individual regeneration," the idea of internal, personal reform that first attracted, then repulsed Orestes Brownson. It is the dogma that allows, and derives from, Channing's capacity to imagine individuals spiritually free while imprisoned in a material world. If his social utterances are not easy to read today, it is because they do not deny this paradox. They virtually celebrate it, and thus defy the common assumptions of Marxists, Skinnerians, and every other variation of modern determinist. Channing's social program may, however, slowly shed its air of quaintness—even today there are signs—as the failure of twentieth-century liberalism gains wider proclamation, and as the repeated degeneration of socialist idealism into totalitarian reality sanctions both an unembarrassed dog-eat-dog capitalist ethic and a soft individualism that can soberly say: society should cater to souls before stomachs.

Much of the present difficulty in taking Channing's social writings seriously stems from his willful ignoring of change. In 1840 his vision of social reality remains static and hierarchical, as if Andrew Jackson had never come east, and John Quincy Adams—"eminent," "venerable . . . [still] . . . at the head of the public men of the country,"[30]—had never left the White House for the House of Representatives. One of the conceptual leaps that Darwin would demand, and that Channing's generation was largely unwilling to make, was to accept the idea of extinction of a species. Following Jefferson, who "reasoned that the mammoth must exist somewhere since his bones had been found,"[31] the rationalist mind required such a literal doctrine of conservation. The great chain of being, which was immutable and sacred, gripped the imagination largely because it allowed a privative idea of evil, allowed, that is, a definition of evil as incompleteness. To abandon such a solace would be to open the floodgates of moral chaos. In the social sphere, Channing is equally unwilling to face that onslaught. Reiterating in 1838 that men are destined to stay in the station into which they are born, he seems to forget that Jackson's disciple occupies the White House, a man who based his politics as much as Jackson had on "the rise of the common man."[32] Indeed Channing pointedly deflates presidential prestige in view of its usurpation by the rabble: "The result of the next election of President . . . [is] . . . insignificant, compared with the great question [of labor]." This may be truth, but it is also self-persuasion. Indeed Channing's conception of political reality, like his social assumptions, may date back to Richmond days. He bears less relation to Van Buren than to Calhoun: "I do not desire [the working man] to struggle into another rank," is almost a disingenuous understatement; what he does desire is a rather Arnoldian process of self-culture—complete with an Arnoldian (and Hopkinsian) vocabulary that long predates *Culture and Anarchy* (1869)— that will sweeten long hours and plain food, and enforce the equation of ambition with absurdity. "I know but one elevation of a human being, and that is Elevation of Soul," and "One thing above all is needful . . . Disinterestedness."[33] In dreaming of such voluntary harmonies, Channing draws on the assumptions about human nature that always underlie Unitarian doctrine: All men are wholly formed but most are half-expressive; felicity must be extracted, not imposed. Like Bronson Alcott's, his pedagogy is interrogative: "Teach much," he counsels, "by questions."[34]

But the questions must provoke only spiritual yearnings. Discontent on earth is, in effect, psychologically treatable, and the displacement of time to a future state is a key step in the therapy: "We must not think of Heaven as a stationary community . . . I think of it, as a society passing through successive stages of development."[35] The "I think" speaks volumes. There was a time in America when ministers did not vacillate in their pictures of judgment.

One cannot, then, properly speak of a temporal world in Channing's thought, as he so variously declines to contend with earthly mutability, preferring to distance it, spiritualize it, disarm it. The means by which he seeks this victory for aloofness is to enclose time in the individual consciousness, adopting a deliberate tunnel vision, concentrating on the growth of one soul while shutting out the multitude. In the larger frame of nineteenth-century individualism this is hardly surprising, but what needs to be seen is its origin in recoil. It is not so much a positive embrace of the autonomous soul as a flight into the mappable terrain of the single mind. Without a critic's coercion, no man is a true bellwether for a century, and Channing may not always place his hand consciously on the pulse of the age. But through him one can vividly feel the careening tempo of the early industrial years.

He makes his return to the individual for the sake of a man's opacity. It is a retirement into a quiet room, away from the heat and light of social change. His relief in the seclusion of the individual mind tells much about the direction of American Protestantism; it could not be more precisely opposite the vision of certain predecessors—once again this is Edwards on the cosmic function of a man: "As God delights in his own beauty he

must necessarily delight in the creature's holiness; which is a
conformity to and participation of it, as truly as the brightness
of a jewel held in the sun's beams."[36] What occurred in the
hundred years between this utterance and Channing's maturity
was a vast reversal in the orientation of the New England mind,
or perhaps more accurately, the triumph of Edwards's
opponents. Emerson, dissenting from the victors, would retrieve
Edwards's jewel and call it an eyeball. Even before the last great
works on *The Nature of True Virtue* (1765) and *The End for
Which God Created the World* (1765), Edwards had located the
beauty of a man in his transparency. His famous metaphor
matching the saint with the rainbow states an ecstatic
accommodation between the two realities to which he was most
sensitive, depravity and beauty: "In the saints . . . dwells no
good thing; they have no light or brightness in them, but only
what is immediately from heaven, from the Sun of
righteousness."[37] For Channing, though he writes in the
seed-time of romanticism, the beauty of a man has become his
capacity to block and frustrate the flow of nature, to resist the
current of history, to siphon what energy he needs and discard
the rest—not his capacity to open himself to God.

Among his most moving sermons, however, is the Edwardsean *Likeness to God* (1828), an embrace of nature and divine
effusion, from which he would retreat during the next decade.
The beauty of that sermon is a strong testimony to his divided
needs. Through these denials he reveals his intellectual root-
lessness. Edwards's assent through man to God is foreclosed
to him; it is more and more necessary for him to separate the
two, to pay them divided homage. To his own century too, as
his wish for insularity shows, he is a partial stranger: "Within,
beyond and beside the old institutions, " Karl Barth has written
of Channing's age, "one must seek to find the proper, true,
living, invisible community."[38] This is not a definition of the
Congregational ideal, though it could be; nor a description of

Edwards's repudiation of his grandfather's polity, though it could be; it is rather a description of the associationism that grew in the early years of the nineteenth century, the epidemic protest that men *could* challenge their given station, that they could link themselves in voluntary union. This too, part of the revolution of his times, Channing distrusted: "I do not approve [Robert] Owen's means; he would accomplish [his end] by merging the individual in the community. I would do it by increasing the power of the individual."[39] The battle lines between the one and the many are drawn.

"[His] thinking, though realistic in a moral sense, and though sometimes enriched by a peculiar kind of imagery, always tends to state social processes in terms of abstract logical developments or to project mythological personifications; he almost never perceives ordinary human beings." Edmund Wilson wrote these words, startlingly appropriate for Edwards, about a great exponent of men's freedom to re-form themselves. Karl Marx was working in the British Museum while Channing preached self-culture—the kind of inviolate individuality that Wilson goes on to say "actually concealed the interests of the petty bourgeois."[40] Indeed, Arminian individualism, of which Channing is a late exponent, had concealed precisely the same interests a century before; this is Channing's most prestigious progenitor, Charles Chauncy, accusing Edwards of straight and simple communism: "[Enthusiasm] is the genuine source of infinite evil . . . It has made strong attempts to destroy all property, to make all things common, *wives* as well as *goods*."[41] The opponents of Edwards (or of the awakeners whom Edwards legitimized) and the opponents of Marx recoil, roughly speaking, from the same perceived threat. This egalitarian strain in evangelical Protestantism has been profoundly explored by Christopher Hill for the seventeenth century and by Alan Heimert for the eighteenth. Like these historians after him and like Chauncy before him, Channing saw the radical writing on the wall.

He is in fact not beyond exploiting the growing insecurity of propertyholders for persuasive purposes. In the antislavery polemics he employs a distinction between natural and legal ownership that plays on the fears of propertied men: that "property is a creature of law" is an intolerable notion, for "according to this doctrine, I see not why the majority, who are always comparatively poor, may not step into the mansions and estates of the rich. I see not why the law cannot make some idle neighbour the rightful owner of your fortune or mine. What better support can Radicalism ask than this?"[42] Turning the order-conserving doctrine of Henry Clay upside down, Channing uses it to brandish a picture of social upheaval—free your slaves to protect yourselves. It is a crafty rhetoric.

As Perry Miller has pointed out, the development of American law through the first half of the nineteenth century necessarily involved evolutionary ideas as legal thinkers sought to describe a domestic line of descent to counter accusations that foreign dictates were swamping the native common law.[43] To authenticate the native precedents meant to risk moral relativism. Thus the development of the legal mind enacts much the same drama that Channing does: a wavering between confidence in the authority of history and a fear that history merely regularizes moral chaos, severing ideas from anything absolute. Indeed Channing expresses a repeated wariness before the law and those who invoke and practice it (apparently unmitigated by his friendship for Joseph Story). The law has suffered degradation, he argues, in the world of slavery apologetics, and its very language has been cheapened to a point of uselessness; a slave ship can be protected or seized merely according to the whim of the legal interpreters. The arbiter for Channing remains English precedent: "the English nation . . .

pronounces the pretended right of property in men an aggravated wrong." But he senses that the idea of self-powered evolution—not instruction from without—will more and more dominate not only the geology and zoology of the planet but also the life of the mind, sanctioning "those evasions, which will do for a court of law, but [not for] a great nation."[44] Precedent, it seemed, could legitimize anything.

In his halt before Owenism and incipient Darwinism, his transformation of self-interest into moral indignation, his deferral of time beyond this world, his doctrine of self-culture, and his circumvention of the implications of America's history—in all these, Channing seeks to hold a crumbling position. Conceiving of virtue as a property of individual insularity, he is ill at ease with the communitarian metaphysics of Edwards, who always conceived of virtue in terms of relation. Equally appalled by the communitarian politics that would culminate in Marx, Channing is caught between one age and another, trying to build something more than a way-station between them.

If located strictly between negatives—between a loathed past and a feared future—the escape into historical immunity might generate some sort of mental rest. But Channing's dilemma is unrelieved and compounded, for he finds attraction as well as repulsion in time. Unitarian moralism, as much as Puritan piety, demands an idea of progress; the idea of regression is anathema—though inherent—to both. A small but revealing sign of Channing's persistence in this New England attitude is his use of the precious Puritan word "type." Though freed from its exclusively exegetical function, and though held back from the broadly applied meaning into which Edwards released it, it retains for Channing the idea of germination, of temporal unfolding: "the mind within me is a type," he declares in 1840, "because my own spirit contains the germs of these [divine] attributes."[45]

In self-contemplation and always, Channing inclines to the value of growth and human connectedness; this is why his apprehension of the perils of time is so deeply trying. Of course the New England mind had never traced history through an unbroken vertical; the outpouring of jeremiad literature well into the eighteenth century flows from the assumption that darkness not only may sometimes precede light but usually does. The blackest times bespeak the imminence of light: for Edwards, the manic suicide of a good Northampton citizen betrays Satan's desperation.[46] Indeed the very origins of America's self conceived millennial role may be traced to the ideology of seventeenth-century Englishmen who accounted for centuries of Catholic rule as a trial of spiritual conditioning and for the short reign of Queen Mary as a not-so-freakish break in the reunion of Britain with her true Protestant self.[47] By 1830 the accommodation of cyclical change into a progressive view of history already had long precedent in America; it had been built into the nation's founding. Channing inherits it, as do the romantic historians whose vision he does not share and who are further confirmed by their reading of the German philosophers.[48] With the early Protestant reformers, with Milton, and even with the romantics themselves in their transposition of religious truth from institution to the human heart, Channing shares the paradox of progressive primitivism—a yearning for advance to simpler days and simpler living. The conspicuous primitivism of the evangelical clergy in the 1840s may have complicated Channing's own leaning in that direction, but however reluctant he may have been to ally with them in this respect, he readily conforms to Richard Hofstadter's description of the revivalists themselves: "The goal of the devout . . . was not to preserve form but to strike anew in order to recapture . . . purity."[49] Channing's most Emersonian utterances echo this conviction;

"Woe to that church; which looks round for forms to wake it up for spiritual life."[50] The urge to reverse, or erase, history cuts across the dividing line between the evangelicals and their critic.

To speak of the Old Testament as "adapted to the childhood of the human race"[51] is to claim adulthood, but also to betray nostalgia. It was, after all, in the childhood of man that Christ consented to speak through miracles, a language that pulverized doubt—a power that Channing would gladly wield over contemporary skeptics and even over the doubting part of his own mind. It is exactly here, in the interregnum between original faith and the laborious exertions of the post-Enlightenment Christian to recapture it, that time becomes an intellectual problem. For time, to put it crudely, is what modern man has had plenty of. To convert those intervening centuries from an endless dry spell into a history of growth, Channing must somehow construe time itself as a gracious gift of God. And so he tries.

Basic to the attempt is the transferral of supremacy from momentary illumination to accumulated wisdom. Less vicious than Orville Dewey toward revivalists, Channing still substantially agrees that conversion is "the slowest of all processes."[52] Indeed the death of Christ himself is a statement of faith in time, for Channing cannot accept the reading of the crucifixion as appeasement of God's wrath. Such raw anger baffles him. Commencing a long lesson, Christ's act of redemption must be instrumental; it is essentially nothing more than an example—excruciating, but an example nevertheless. The history of man, then, is a history of education. Lessons need to be unlearned; these are the historical reversals. And these conclusions carry a poignancy of self-reference: "As men advance in civilization," he says at the close of the great Dudleian lecture of 1821, "they become susceptible of mental sufferings, to which ruder ages are strangers." If sometimes a touch disingenuous, sometimes faint-hearted, and often at a loss, Channing is always profoundly civilized and aware (unlike many of his rising countrymen) that civilization can bring exactly the opposite of ease. Christ, he asserts, knew it too: "The fitness of our religion to more advanced stages of society than that in which it was introduced, to wants of human nature not then developed, seems to me very striking. The religion bears the marks of having come from a being who perfectly understood the human mind, and had power to provide for its progress. This feature of Christianity is of the nature of prophecy. It was an anticipation of future and distant ages; and, when we consider among whom our religion sprung, where, but in God, can we find an explanation of this peculiarity?"[53] Time lies at the heart of God's dispensation. To lose the sense of history is to blaspheme.

The necessity of time for the fulfillment of human destiny, and a consequent human obligation to exercise patience, become doctrines for Channing. With them, he treads near again to a faith derived by a process of elimination—and the last straw man to be knocked down is invariably the kind of man who scorns the claims of Christian history, the Jew. As the future will be characterized by a breakdown of national distinctions,[54] so the past, particularly the Jewish past, was closed, circumscribed by the arrogance of self-interest and the idiocy of "chosenness." This is a significant conjunction in American intellectual history—the conviction that human progress will constitute a superseding of the Jewish mentality, an idea with which Henry Adams and T.S. Eliot would later concur. In Channing's case, it may have been heightened by his recollection of Newport as an unholy mix of reprobates, including an unusual number of Jews—several hundred in a city of ten thousand—who so seeped into respectable circles that even Ezra Stiles marched on holidays with the rabbis, absorbing "the mysteries of the Cabala."[55] These notions may not properly be called the seeds of genteel antisemitism in America; they are rather a young shoot, for anti- and philosemitism had grown together in New England since the founding. An identification with Israel had crossed the Atlantic with Winthrop's generation, emerging in the same culture that obsessively condemned the failure of the Jews to read Old Testament types—persons and events that anticipate the life and messages of Christ—as harbingers of gospel truth. Repeating this refrain fostered self-hatred, since New Englanders likened themselves to the nation they condemned.

It is this double legacy that Channing adopts and modifies. "Whilst all other men are formed in a measure by the spirit of the age, we can discover in Jesus no impression of the period in which he lived."[56] Throughout Channing's thought there runs a stream of antiprovincialism, and this solemn praise of Christ's historical "immunity" is a main tributary. To be honestly evaluated, such praise of ecumenism—a widely shared tenet of the Unitarians[57]—must be seen in its proper context; as a manifestation of the provincial intellectual's claim to urbanity, as a form of self-exoneration after a decade of ecclesiastical strife for which the Unitarians were largely responsible, and as a conscious prelude to disowning the Transcendentalist mutiny. The Unitarians, in short, claimed to rise above their time and place. And they shook their heads at family squabbles: "Sects are apt to hate each other in proportion to their proximity." But such words inevitably achieve irony in light of the feuding in which American Unitarianism was born. Liberal and orthodox churches were notable for both hatred and proximity; it was not uncommon for the scaffolding of a splinter church to rise within sight of the original. The gentle latitudinarianism so often cred- ited to Channing's movement cloaks a sentiment of self-congrat- ulation for a spirit of tolerance. "[Christ] was a Jew, and the first and deepest and most constant impression on a Jew's mind, was that of the superiority conferred on his people."[58] Such rational antisemitism, as so often in America, conceals a component of self-hatred, for the conceptual enemy is the provincial, while the Christian hero is he who rises above his historical milieu—a parallel, perhaps unconscious, for the postrevolutionary New England intellectual, proudly, but nervously, independent of his English home. But more than providing a conceptual underpinning for bigotry, this mode of thinking strengthens what is perhaps the most deeply conservative strand of rational religious thought: the conviction that sudden shifts in history are monumental phenomena, to be noted, revered, and held high above unassisted human emulation. In a once current vocabulary Channing would be called a premillennial thinker (again the opposite of Edwards). For him real change implies cataclysm. It did not, and will not arise organically through the process of history; man must await divine fiat. In the cruder minds of other liberal apologists, the longer the wait, the better. All this is precisely analogous to the position on miracles; God interrupts the natural law in order to rivet man's attention, humble him, sustain his faith, and equally to discourage him from expecting miracles to recur in anything but the gravest extremity. Christ was delivered to such an age of extremity. William Lloyd Garrison was not.

Channing invests a great deal in the momentousness of historical interruption. The extraworldly origin of Christianity itself is another defense, albeit a negative one, of faith. One should recall his remarkably defensive credo: "I believe Christianity to . . . have come from God, because it seems to me impossible to trace it to any other origin." His is a faith that feeds on the extraordinary and starves on the usual. Again manifesting the provincial's anxiety, he objects to the kind of complacency that translates the usual into law. Contemporary skeptics may have been sophisticates, but Channing's version of the agnostic is a narrowly experienced man, a man who argues that since many miracles have been superstitious illusions, all must be. His impatience is not with the scientific view so much as with the quasi-scientific mind, with the layman lulled into false ease by the currency of scientific jargon. The rules of supply and demand, of Newport shipping and Boston trade, follow the odds of percentages, not the laws of mathematics. Only in the small mind does the ordinary exclude the exception. Indeed the whole defense of miracles may be seen as an effort to save the possibility of escape from routine, from deadening habit, from American life itself. It is a plea that the world can be different from what it has been.[59]

Channing invests at least as much, if not more, in the rarity of the antihistorical event. God acts sparingly; his intervention would be cheapened by repetition. This is the heart of conservatism: "Multitudes, unwilling to wait the slow pace of that great innovator, time, are taking the work of reform into their own hands."[60] Faced with abolitionist fury, Channing overcomes his discomfort about time and deifies its regular process, exactly that from which he has recoiled. Indeed he flinches at every disruption in the steady flow, and his antipathy to abruptness weakens the moral force of his endorsements. A growing motive behind his antislavery position, for example, is his perception that the continuance of slavery would lead to greater social upheaval than would its termination. His awareness of such a mixture of motives, and its relevance to his idea of truth, will make slavery the test of his life.

The loss of epistemological and existential confidence between New England's early generations and Channing's is clearly signaled in the confrontation with time. How gladly would Channing say, with one of the early Puritans, that "time is one of the most precious blessings which worthless man in this world enjoys; a jewel of inestimable worth; a golden stream, dissolving, and as it were, continually running down by us, out of one eternity into another."[61] But he cannot say it. The great dilemma of this sometimes foundering man is to reconcile a need for progress with a need for rest. Sometimes weakened by that dual wish, he is driven into intellectual strategies that yield weak moral consequences. But the lapses proclaim his humanity, and are collectively redressed in his brave and insistent distinction between the human and the bestial: "To the animal, the past is a blank, and so is the future. The present is every thing. But to the mind the present is comparatively nothing."[62] "No mind," Dr. Johnson had said through Imlac, "is much employed upon the present; recollection and anticipation fill up almost all our moments."[63] Consider the concern, often unformed but always silently subversive, of a man who would stay in the comforting fellowship of Johnson, but who must confess that the "feverish Present swallows up men's thoughts."[64] For "the feverish present" more and more fills Channing's consciousness, until he must speak, in the paean to sleep, of man's "animal frame." Immersed in the present, married to nature, man is blurring the distinction between himself and the unreasoning beasts. In Channing's darker moods—intimidated both by the backward leap through memory and by a forward push through political action—he feels that distinction almost beyond recall.

3

Language and the Neutrality of Scripture

Experience proves surely that the Bible does not answer a purpose for which it was never intended. It may be accidentally the means of the conversion of individuals; but a book, after all, cannot make a stand against the wild living intellect of man, and in this day it begins to testify, as regards its own structure and contents, to the power of that universal solvent, which is so successfully acting upon religious establishments.

—John Henry Cardinal Newman

A RANCOROUS, if secondary, historical debate in recent years has concerned the place of the Bible in American religion. Broadly speaking, it has long been assumed that scriptural authority rather quickly disappeared under the combined weight of the Enlightenment and the higher criticism, but that before its collapse, for nearly two centuries, doctrinal controversy was conducted by men who agreed on the court of final appeal while disputing its verdict. That scripture in the nineteenth century had lost its centrality has not been much denied. Dickinson, Whitman, Thoreau all felt the need to make their own holy book. To them at least, the old one was defunct. But the unbroken dominance of scripture in the previous two centuries has not been so cordially agreed upon. Perhaps the sharpest blow to the idea of such servility in colonial America, to the idea that American theologians needed Griesbach and Strauss to pry them loose from the Bible, was dealt by Perry Miller thirty years ago. Miller's readings of Jonathan Edwards as a man variously in advance of his time elicited fierce, even savage rebuttals, works with barbed titles like *Loss of Mastery* and "The Modernity of Jonathan Edwards," responses designed to return Edwards to the position of anachronistic fundamentalist in which V. L. Parrington had left him in the 1920s.[1] In order to feel the full impact of the question of scripture for Channing and his generation, it is necessary, if only briefly, to take sides in this debate. To put it simply, it makes a difference whether the Baltimore sermon, in which Channing set forth the liberals' principles for reading the Bible, is regarded as a pioneer departure from scripture, as many have read it, or as a reduction of scriptural authority, not original but different in kind from one that came before.

"Liberal" is a hard word to keep from loose usage. Though hardly the same thing, political and religious liberalism are often confused, and exegetical liberalism falls easily into the conglomerate. The basis upon which Miller subverted such historical and ideological assumptions and threw into question the triplet birth of these forms of liberalism in the early nineteenth century is the fact that the most puritan of America's eighteenth-century ministers was able to read the Bible with considerable latitude as early as 1758. Here, for example, Edwards catalogues a half-dozen meanings of "glory," not in order to fix its definition, but to loosen it:

> Let us begin with the phrase, *The Glory of God* . . . it is sometimes used to signify the second person in the Trinity . . . the root it comes from, is . . . the verb . . . which signifies *to be heavy* . . . sometimes it is used to signify what is *internal, inherent,* or in the possession of the person: and sometimes for *emanation, exhibition,* or *communication* of this internal glory: and sometimes for the *knowledge,* or *sense* of these, in those to whom the exhibition or communication is made . . . When the word is used to signify what is within . . . it very commonly signifies *excellency,* dignity, or worthiness or regard . . .[2]

Near the end of his life, Edwards is draining the opacity out of the words in much the same way that he rendered transparent the image of man. His favorite scriptural passages are metaphorical, his favorite words abstract—"union," "relation"—like empty vessels to be filled by the seepage from words around them. The reader is called to look not closely at words, but through words toward God. Fixity of meaning no longer holds Edwards's interest; he delights in the range of meanings, in the variety rather than the stability of God's language. The insight that allows Edwards to risk this liberation is what Miller called "the vision of a universe organized around the act of perception."[3] The human senses are the conduits of grace; what distinguishes the saint is that he sees, hears, feels the good, not the way he defines the terms of an argument, even a scriptural argument. Long before the higher criticism, Jonathan Edwards could accept the imprecision of translation, the unreliability of text collation, the accretion of corrupt variants, since apprehension of the divine depended not on correctness but on the immediate imparting of true sight from God to man. Through a phrase of many grammatical meanings, the saint always sees God; through a phrase of fixed meaning, the unregenerate man sees nothing, except perhaps himself. For Edwards the mediate object, whether a passage from Revelation or a flowering elm, will always reveal its full beauty to those who can see and will always remain a gaggle of words or a pretty tree to those who cannot. The heart of the matter is in the beholder.

The reasons that impelled Channing to undercut scriptural infallibility fifty years later were very different. If Edwards moved with confidence in the inviolable connection between God and man, Channing and his colleagues moved with deep insecurity, less in celebration than in flight from an old house collapsing. The Unitarians, in the end, committed themselves to living in a world of ambiguity between two worlds of clarity, the orthodox and the romantic. And they knew it. For one thing they were constantly being reminded how inadequate was their vision for a creature poised before death. Samuel Miller of Princeton put the charge neatly into an anecdote: " 'I should like,' said one of the shrewdest men in our country, on being asked, after his return from hearing the most popular Unitarian preacher then in Boston, how he was pleased with him, 'I should like,' said he, 'always to hear such preaching, if I were sure I was never to die.' "[4] Familiarity did not dull the blow; as we shall see, Channing grew increasingly sensitive to the justice in this sarcasm, and his rising awareness made him quieter rather than louder in defense of liberal principles. More and more of his energy went toward refuting the charge "that we are guilty of base compliances, and of shunning to declare the whole counsel of God from regard to human applause."[5] Channing could not turn back to the synthesis of revealed law and scriptural promise, nor would he move fully forward into romantic internalization and naturalization of the divine. He could not stay with the written law of God, and he would not allow its transformation into instinct. To see how he coped with his double refusal is to see both his predicament and his strength.

The election of Henry Ware to the Hollis Professorship at Harvard in 1805 is usually cited as the real outbreak of liberal-orthodox warfare. Like all such historical markers, it is only a convenience, but it serves. Still, the fame of the date obscures the fact that the real polemics did not get under way until ten years later. In 1815, Jedidiah Morse's periodical, *The Panoplist*, published a long article charging conspiracy and dissembling among the liberal clergy. Usually conciliatory, Channing felt compelled to answer. He did not expect that his *Letter to Samuel Thacher* (1815) would generate two rebuttals and require two sequels. It was the largest public controversy in which he would participate until slavery.

When the Harvard Board of Overseers split almost down the middle over Ware's election, the fight seemed clear: doctrines were at stake. Depravity, atonement, damnation. One side held them literally sacred, the other hedged. Most modern accounts still stress the doctrinal disputes,[6] and of course they were essential—but it is necessary to probe beneath them to find the roots of bitterness.

Hearing the orthodox fury, one feels witness even today to a racking anguish—for though the surface of Morse's *True Reasons on which the Election of a Hollis Professor was Opposed* (1805) is snappish and impatient with liberal evasion, its deeper tone is one of fear at the subversion of everything stable in the world: "Now if barriers so sacred can be removed, what guard can be devised, which shall secure any bequest against violation?"[7] Morse is speaking specifically of Thomas Hollis's right to expect his survivors to stop the dissipation of his fortune to those who count Jesus merely first among men and who consider sin an excess of appetite. Hollis has a sacred right, insists Morse, to support godly men in the Chair that bears his name, and godly men believe none of the things that Henry Ware believes. But the real plea is not concerned with individuals, nor even points of doctrine. It is to save the fading conviction that truth remains stable through time, to recall that men commit the sin of pride in refining the gospel in accordance with their temperament. For Morse, 1805 was a year of fantastic insolence; like children of a senile parent, the liberal ministry were living off Hollis's income while chuckling at his incontinence.

The accession of Ware, then, was scandalous, but Morse and his allies felt the liberals to be less brats than fools. "I could smile," Channing wrote in 1815, "at the idea of a *Unitarian plot*."[8] But if Morse believed him, he found nothing cheering in ingenuousness; whether or not he credited his own charges of plots and secret strategies is really beside the point. For a child, he knew, can be more destructive in his innocence of obligations than in his guile to shirk them: the world was going to hell without knowing it.

Leading the way were those who would sabotage New England's institutions. It was finally over the future of institutional integrity that New England split to the core. Morse's concern was to save Harvard College from the infidel present; the Unitarians' was to use the present to nullify the past. This is the opposition that dominates the period.

When Channing joined the fray ten years after the Ware dispute, he came as a peacemaker: "We esteem it a solemn duty to disarm instead of exciting the bad passions of our people."[9] But the orthodox camp, speaking now through Samuel Worcester, refused the truce: "Did the apostles, then, studiously avoid controversy?" A few pages after posing that loaded question, Worcester speaks to the heart of the conflict: "Already, alas! [the idea is] too prevalent that truth is not worth contending for."[10] His phrasing is perhaps unwarranted, but his point is inescapable to anyone who reads through the Unitarian position papers of the teens and twenties. Not only does their constant iteration of pacific hopes and goodwill drive it home, but it becomes evident that they themselves came to realize they had no fortress to defend. At best they had a method.

And so it is not surprising to find Ezra Stiles Gannett still preaching thirty years after Ware's appointment on *Christian Unitarianism Not a Negative System*, a work in which an early paragraph contains nine repetitions of "we believe." But catalogued articles of faith could not carry the day. There is no ignoring the fact that the liberal-orthodox fight was at bottom a conflict between historicism and a faith in revealed truth. The orthodox mind simply could not conceive that the quality of flexibility has anything to do with truth; it could not tolerate skepticism in the house of belief: "To believe in *The Innocence of Error* . . . is what I call *Indifference to Truth.*"[11]

What Morse failed to articulate, though the recognition hovers on the edge of his polemic, is that the liberals equally could never grasp his argument for the sanctity of institutions—whether a Harvard College Chair or a restricted communion—because they had abandoned the idea of truth as a static thing, a thing that could be embodied in institutional form.[12] Accordingly, the response of men like Gannett to the charge that liberalism broke down systems while never building them up was to remind the orthodox of their reformation origins. The terms of the debate forced both parties to conceive of New England's churches as beleaguered cathedrals. Eventually the Transcendentalists would have their revenge by dubbing Andrews Norton a pope—while Orestes Brownson, who consigned them all to perdition, cried "Protestantism is no-churchism . . . no positive religion," and fled to Rome.[13]

The horrified recoil of the orthodox from what they considered shameless relativism is a hard thing for modern liberals to view with sympathy. "Fisher Ames," wrote Parrington, "[was] mightily concerned that the future should be as like the past as one generation of oysters is like another."[14] There is the same kind of stoniness in the orthodox temperament—but we should also be able to feel something more human—an urge to conserve, to hold the place, the habits, the faces, among which we are born. If it is reactionary, it is also a stay against chaos.

Jedidiah Morse may not have been a profoundly insightful man, but he could see that what he called distortion his opponents called progress. He could also see that the removal of authority from institutions would require its transfer somewhere else. When the Unitarians found their younger disciples pointing to their own souls—and even to their bodies—as the new repositories of truth, Morse's fear was realized. After 1805, an Emerson was inevitable.

When Channing published his letter to Thacher, he could not judge the force of the current to which he was committing himself. The history of his defense of liberal exegesis is the history of his gradual recognition of where that current was carrying him. As early as 1808 he spoke out harshly against his fellow clergy, but not, as might be expected, against their Calvinist doctrine. On the contrary, he warned against coddling, against lukewarmness in the pulpit: "Of all the frowns of Providence, perhaps none is more threatening than the settlement of a cold-hearted, uninterested minister. His coldness petrifies all within his influence."[15] As the Puritans in Episcopal England had cried out against a ministry that preached "for fashion sake . . . for ostentation sake . . . for ambition," pronouncing that the only true priestly function was to "Deliver a man from hell," so Channing two centuries later entirely agrees: "A minister has a soul to save, as well as his people . . . of all men, a cold, negligent minister has the darkest prospects."[16] There is nothing complacent in the young Channing. Together with the soul-saving charge of the ministry goes a vivid emphasis on the tenacity of sin—the "fire which is never quenched, . . . [the] worm which never dies."[17] In later years one of the orthodox spokesmen would remind New England liberals that their leader had spoken such words in righteous defense of the faith of their fathers, and another of Channing's critics would appeal to him to recall what "you avowed when you first became a preacher of the gospel."[18]

If three years after the Ware upheaval Channing was preaching music to orthodox ears, where were the seeds of his discontent? Why did he leave the ranks? An answer is contained in the same sermon that blasted the ministry for its ease: "A minister," Channing declared, "must never say that he has formed his system, and has nothing to do but to preach it."[19] Channing was already uneasy with formulas, wary of rote piety, contemptuous of the routine. The crucial point is his determination to escape dependence on an inscribed system—for as the years went on it became less and less possible for him to join the likes of Morse in their homage to tradition. Where they found stability, he found formalism; where they found security, he found suffocation. Thus one can see in Channing even at his most orthodox a looming restlessness. One sees here again that the heart of the schism was not really doctrinal, but temperamental. For Channing could not rest on the past no matter how true he felt it to be. His departure into liberalism was a measure of deep cultural change, as it manifested the need of a new generation to find its own relation to God. The process of developing a personal faith was becoming paramount—even if the ultimate achievement should echo that of their fathers.

When, in the late 1830s, Emerson exalted the same urge for independence, he insisted that the past and present could remain linked without being interdependent: "The American who has been confined, in his own country, to the sight of buildings designed after foreign models, is surprised on entering York Minster or St. Peter's at Rome, by the feeling that these structures are imitations also,—faint copies of an invisible archetype."[20] There was a wonderful comfort in that sense of déjà vu, for Emerson understood the danger in severance from the past as well as the danger in servility to it. Channing, too, had walked between them.

Since he entered the debate long after the furor over Ware had subsided, one must look to a different issue for the evidence of Channing's skepticism toward institutional continuity. Among Worcester's charges, the one that rankled most was the call for separation, with its implicit disgust at contact with a heathen faction. The liberals, Worcester was saying, were unfit to live with. Channing's consequent outrage is partly personal: "Would he not have said," he asks, hypothesizing a reversal of roles, "that I was aiming a blow at what was dearer to him than life, at his Christian character, and his usefulness as a minister?"[21] But like Morse on the election, Channing's response is not finally personal. He addresses rather the intellectual arrogance in the idea of separation itself, and in its repugnance for him we see once more the fundamental cleavage between those who would yield to institutional power and those who could no longer trust it.

Among those who held on, perhaps the most imposing was Lyman Beecher, leader of a major counterattack against the liberal mutiny. The "long and dreadful declension from evangelical doctrine and piety," could be traced, according to Beecher, to "the lax mode of admission to the churches."[22] One must not confuse the orthodox faith in institutions with an allegiance to those of contemporary New England: purification was called for. Beecher's lament, informed by the 1820 Massachusetts Supreme Court ruling that a parish may overrule a church majority in appointing officials,[23] was over the merger of civil and ecclesiastical authority. One may imagine Beecher side by side with Worcester as the target of Channing's passionate question: "Is he sure that he has not been labouring to drive from the Christian fold the friends of Jesus and the heirs of salvation?"[24] That question reveals how far New England had traveled from her origins. If once her ideologues had been prepared to risk excluding a saint from church fellowship in order to keep out the contaminating reprobate, now Channing confesses the hopelessness of such discrimination. It is an admission that God may no longer work through human institutions, and those who subscribed to that admission—as their enemies were quick to tell them—had no right to be surprised when one of their number stood in the Harvard Divinity School and called it a dead shell.

This debate, buried in dry manifestos and drier replies (Channing excluded his contributions from the edition of his collected works), should not be dismissed as arcane. It is one episode in the continuing American contest between the egalitarian idea and the conviction that men should recognize—and judge— the differences between them. The liberal rebellion against the privilege of exclusion is one of the elements that led such historians as Parrington to count the liberals in the democratic vanguard, and there is much wisdom in Parrington's reading. But we must not lose sight of the potential for loneliness, for a feeling of drift and fearful self-reliance, that resides in their rejection of institutional authority. Channing felt the loss, and the critical stage of his thinking came when he contemplated its remedy.

Among the repositories of truth that could no longer be trusted—especially as they were recognized "not to be inspired texts, but rather texts written by inspired men"[25]—were the scriptures. As several scholars have lately pointed out,[26] the harnessing of new philological methods practiced in Germany (most conspicuously by Andrews Norton in his massive *Evidences of the Genuineness of the Gospels,* 1837-44) was doomed to undermine its own purpose. Rather than stabilizing scripture by cleaning away its internal discrepancies, the new scholarship brought home the fact of human authorship, thus exposing the Bible to exactly the same suspicions that the liberals had expressed toward church, toward university, toward every man-made receptacle with claims to containing God's truth.

But lest exclusive attention be granted to what we may call the problem of scripture as an institution, it must be acknowledged that there were other reasons for Channing's wariness before the sacred text. To put it simply, the Bible said some things that were unwelcome to the Unitarian-Federalist frame of mind. "Unitarians . . . shudder when they hear . . . that the ever blessed God suffered and died on the cross."[27] The crucified Christ has always been a troublesome image for Christian rationalists, not only because the doctrine of atonement all but prohibits rebellion against the doctrine of depravity but also because the image makes its essential appeal not to reason, but to passion.[28]Channing, as we have seen in his responses to nature, to Napoleon, to Jackson, was profoundly wary of such appeal—

conscious as he was of its susceptibility to abuse. Federalist scorn for the mob is a well-known refrain from these years, and Channing was hardly free of it. "Barbarous phraseology," he declared, "is the chief wall of partition [between the Unitarians and Trinitarians]," and though he never conceded the point, one detects a concern that some of that barbarism afflicts scripture itself. "All this," the vision of God bleeding and spit upon, "is theology of man's making," and "Who does not know, that man will attach himself most strongly to the God who has become a man?"[29] He could not associate himself with the divine authorization of that union.

Upon this dissent Channing built his interpretation of scripture. It was not enough to expunge the offending passages; the list was too long: "Nothing is easier than to produce a string of texts in support of every doctrine."[30] The need was more radical, and to meet that need Channing spelled out the principles of rational exegesis in the Baltimore sermon. In essence, he claimed that scripture demands the employment of reason to arbitrate its contradictory statements, and to qualify its imperatives by reconstructing the time and place from which they were delivered. It was a simple enough program—ultimately the same as Joseph Story's principles for reading the Constitution. It was clear. And it was unbearable to the orthodox.

The explosive that Channing brandished was, like so many elements of this debate, more threatening in what it might lead to than in itself. For the insistence on reason in interpretation boiled down to the idea that man must supply the key without which scripture was gibberish, or worse, without which it might seem to make an unintended sense. It is here that we see most clearly the affinity with Edwards; and to see that kinship is to go some distance toward comprehending what happened to New England religion after the century turned. For Edwards too had granted the existence of a requisite key: his was individually God-given, the indwelling spirit of discernment. Channing's key, except for his more strenuous assertion that it could be dup-licated and handed out to any man, is not so different. Finding himself utterly dependent upon the individual perception, he was stymied, for he did not share Edwards's serene belief in God's sublime orchestration of all men into a great march toward redemption. Channing found himself with nowhere to turn but inward—in an age that Locke had taught to look for truth from without. Some men, Channing had to concede, would be good readers of scripture, others bad. The world had broken into millions of churches of one.

His opponents saw the explosion. They saw that an un-bridgeable gap had opened for some New Englanders between individual conscience and scriptural authority. Preaching against the war in 1812, Channing had linked the two stumbling blocks, incitement to rebellion against the standing order, and the sanction of an immoral relation between men: "Civil commotion should be viewed as the worst of national evils, with the single exception of slavery."[31] Of course there is political retaliation in the joining of this pair of evils, but the balance of his life confirms the authenticity of Channing's disgust at slavery, and that disgust inevitably fell between him and scripture. "On the ground of two or three passages," he wrote in an antislavery pamphlet of the 1830s, "we make Christianity the minister of slavery . . . Of what avail are a few texts, which were designed for local and temporary use, when urged against the vital, essential spirit, and the plainest precepts of our religion?"[32] In hearing this dismissal of the Pauline epistles as "a few texts," one might recall how a few lines of Genesis 17—"I will establish my covenant between me and thee and thy seed after thee"—had once provided a basis for the self-image of all New England, an idea of covenant that lasted at least a hundred years.

Chief among those of his opponents who recognized Chan-ning's dilemma was Moses Stuart of Andover. Stuart addressed

a series of letters to Channing in 1819 (immediately after the
Baltimore sermon) that make a moving call for the prodigal to
return before it is too late: "At *present* you do not avow or
defend such opinions [as the Germans' skepticism]. A short time
since they did not." The power of Stuart's plea remains
considerable today because he was not an antiquated man. His
command of the relevant languages and the latest advances in
scriptural studies rivaled Andrews Norton's, and he was frank
about his self-restraint: "My investigation must be conducted
independently of my *philosophy,* by my *philology.*"[33] He was
frank too about his consistency: one finds him defending the
Fugitive Slave Act in 1850, long after others had found ways of
skirting the Pauline sanction of slavery.[34] Stuart preached the
courage of self-suppression. Like Morse, but more brilliantly, he
defended absolutes as necessary for civilized human intercourse.
In the process, he found himself including plantations as well as
universities among those worthy of defense. And in the effort he
made it very clear that he did not feel estranged from the modern
world, nor did he concede that such estrangement was necessary
to keep the faith: "We affirm . . . that gravitation brings a body,
which is thrown into the air, down to earth. The fact is altogether intelligible. The terms are perfectly understood, so far as
they are employed to describe this fact. But then *what is* gravitation? An affirmative definition cannot be given, which is not a
mere exchange of synonymes."[35] Stuart insisted that modern
science tolerates—indeed depends upon—exactly the same
imprecision that religion demands. He enlists the full force of his
argument in defense of the trinity—the inexplicable one in
three—but the idea of impenetrable mystery is not a defensive
ploy; it is central to the age. Stuart is asking that man consent to
live with metaphor, that he resist his urge to analyze, or as a
contemporary put it, to "murder to dissect." The crisis he anticipated was vividly experienced by Channing, for Channing did

need the mysteries that he discarded, did need the truth beyond the reach of reason, even as he turned away from it.

Moses Stuart wanted Channing to recognize a distinction between "*terms* which are unintelligible, and *things* which are undefinable."[36] When one reads the works that document Channing's turn toward the liberals, one sometimes feels that he could have gone either way, but the indignity of surrender to institutionalized mystery proved too much for him. "If reason be so dreadfully darkened by the fall," he said in Baltimore, "that its most decisive judgments on religion are unworthy of trust, then Christianity, and even natural theology, must be abandoned; for the existence and veracity of God, and the divine original of Christianity, are conclusions of reason, and must stand or fall with it."[37] Channing spoke in Baltimore of man's obligation to satisfy his need for self-determination—a phrase that Edwards had called nonsensical, and one that we know today only as a euphemism for military aid to despots.

The best minds among the orthodox understood that they were witnessing a major triumph of individualism. Like Stuart, Leonard Woods of Andover sought to forestall the confusion of orthodoxy with antimodernism. He dexterously employed the precedents of Bacon and Newton in his call to reason from the facts spelled out by scripture rather than fit the facts to some preconceived hypothesis about the nature of God: "this principle [of induction] is as applicable to the science of *theology*, as to the science of *physics*." If Stuart's premonitions warned mainly of skepticism, Woods, writing barely a year later, gave primacy to a different danger. "According to the scriptures," he began, "the grand means, by which God will promote the happiness of his kingdom, is the administration of a *moral government*. Such a government implies a law, enforced by proper sanctions."[38] The decay of scripture meant the decay of social order. Still another orthodox spokesman lamented a year later that there was "no longer any uniform standard" but only "licentiousness of interpretation."[39] Woods had already expanded that pessimism before it was uttered; the new licentiousness was not confined to the act of reading. Antinomianism was abroad.

Channing never directly answered the combined attack of Stuart and Woods. One can only speculate why he left that task to Norton and to Henry Ware respectively. Perhaps it was his memory of how his exchange with Worcester had further poisoned the air. If that was his concern, the "Wood 'n' Ware controversy," as contemporaries liked to call it, proved him right. There is new fatigue in their dutiful pages. Woods throws up his hands, content to refute the charge of irrationalism, while the well-meaning Ware merely repeats the irreconcilables—depravity and omnipotence, damnation and God's love—never comprehending that it is precisely these balks at divine mystery that the orthodox call presumption. He cannot understand their call for acceptance of the inscrutability of God.[40]

It may be that Channing's silence meant more than weariness, that he understood what Ware did not. It may be that he saw ominous truth in the orthodox charge that his party had become "deists in disguise."[41] Of course he never had Andrews Norton's taste for combat, a lack that may be called either timidity or an alertness to ambiguity. The evidence of Channing's life sanctions the second explanation.

The middle 1820s were quiet years. Relatively free from discord, Channing used the time to promote the idea of a national literature and to speak on the subject of Milton. It is surely not coincidence that these concerns engaged him hard upon the scripture controversy. As the Bible fell from dominance, it was a kind of substitution to turn toward Milton and to the dream of American Miltons in future years. In 1826 he did preach in New York on *Unitarian Christianity Most Favorable to Piety*, a work that includes what Parrington called "his most dramatic passage,"[42] a vivid attack on the image of the suffering Christ. It is a sermon preached to repel the continuing charges of skeptical and antinomian "tendency" in the Unitarian faith. But apart from such occasional defense, Channing adhered to his earlier claim that "we are not governed by a proselyting temper."[43] It was as if he had put away the mantle that the Baltimore sermon had earned him.

Channing felt himself to be a better man in peace than in war—a confession he would continually make, with diminishing accuracy, as the slavery crisis worsened. All his life, through the legacy of Newport and the lesson of his mother, he was painfully sensitive to insincerity, to duplicity, to pose. And yet his behavior in the factional battles that preceded the 1820s can sometimes disappoint even his admirers. There were lapses, not collapses: "If I were to define the word 'orthodox,' I should say that it means the predominant party in the church, and especially those who are so destitute of humility as to arrogate to themselves an exclusive understanding of the gospel."[44] Channing very well knew that the difference was not in numbers; he is throwing here the *Panoplist* charge of liberal predominance back into the orthodox face. Angered, he was capable even of exploiting scandal: when Worcester claimed that he distorted the Calvinist catechism, Channing allowed himself a broad sarcasm. He would be delighted, he asserts, to find that they did not believe what he thought they believed, but his doctrinal descriptions derive, he regrets, from "Miss Adams' Views of Religion," a compilation by a lady reputed to have accused Jedidiah Morse of plagiarism. It was dirty laundry, nothing more or less, and Channing shyly confined it to an endnote.[45]

More serious than occasional nastiness is the fact that he could lose in the heat of exchange his usual psychological acuity. His response to the dual accusation of Unitarian antipopular elitism and Unitarian thirst for popular "applause" is to labor the contradiction between the charges. He ignores what he knows full well, that prestige may derive from minority appeal even more surely than from the embrace of the masses. There was nothing contradictory between the contention that Unitarians sought to please and Lyman Beecher's remark that "the liberal system . . . has never been the religion of the common people,"[46] and Channing knew it.

He knew in his private times that decency, including his own, could fail under duress. From that recognition, from his fatigue, and from his own awareness of the perils of the departures from authority that he had undertaken, there flowed a longing for conciliation, a hunger for peace.

The desire for repose is a theme unto itself in Channing's thought. But it runs parallel with, and sometimes overlaps, the rather ponderous refrain of many Unitarian apologists that the flexibility of their creed was a measure of its hospitality. In the face of invective, the Unitarian would often offer a seat in his sitting room to the orthodox enemy, claiming that a closer look from without would reveal a friendly host within. "Under the disguise of technical phraseology," Henry Ware, Jr., found most men united at heart, since Unitarianism "occupies the common ground of Christians." Channing agreed: "The differences between Unitarians and Trinitarians lie more in sounds than in ideas."[47]

What may at first seem an unwillingness to face contention is actually a rage to believe that differences arise not finally out of conviction but out of expression. We are in the core of Channing's rationalism when we contemplate his fervor to believe in the essential unity of men who condemn each other daily. This is his precious faith that the world speaks coherently to its human inhabitants, that neither man nor nature requires radical alteration, but that men's way of saying what they see holds the fault. It is this faith that the dark romantics would so bitterly challenge. Poe would propose the novel remedy in "The Domain of Arnheim" (1847) of shifting the therapy from subject to object, while Melville would funnel his anguish through the cabin boy Pip, whose abandonment at sea constricts his speech to one utterance, the conjugation of the verb "to look." Pip will see the world and find it has no center: "I look, you look, he looks; we look, ye look, they look."[48] Channing, accused by his opponents of undermining the center upon which men depend, refuses such radical doubt, but because he feels its approach he alone emerges from the denominational quarrels as an enduring figure in American letters. It is true that he calls "uniformity of opinion" an "airy good,"[49] but the point is easily misunderstood. He does not contend that all disputes are phantom—that would be willful dreaming—but he does insist that under the confusion lies harmony. This is the message of the Baltimore sermon, that if men can regularize the irregularities of scripture, they will find that they agree at heart. To find their brotherhood they must travel beyond the realm of expression.

It is possible to argue, and tempting to do it with irony, that the Unitarians were right in claiming their creed as the lowest common denominator of Christianity. Moses Stuart himself conceded that the liberals had not yet disappeared below the cutoff level into atheism, but another inch downward and there would indeed be "different Gods and different gospels"[50] in the land. It was to fend off that outcome that Channing, against his inclinations, tackled the issues of the doctrinal dispute. His expectations from scripture were not so much that it could vindicate his stance as that he could count on its neutrality: "I do not propose to prove the truth of Unitarianism by Scriptural authorities,"[51] he said, because he doubted it could be done. What permitted him to live with that doubt was an equal skepticism that scripture could seal the victory for his opponents.

This balance of inefficacy, an extraordinary stalemate for its time, illuminates once again Channing's ironic proximity to

Edwards. Like Edwards, he confessed the imprecision of scripture; neither man was a dogmatic reader, neither pounded out
the gist of a disputed phrase. Edwards—to borrow from old
Puritan parlance—could live with matters "indifferent," because
he knew that truth dwelt in the heart, not on the page. For Channing to believe that, he had to grant enormous authority to the
self, and he had to do it in a world much less sure than Edwards's
of God's superintendence. To escape relativism, he found, he
must deify the individual.

As we have already seen, and as the slavery issue would
manifestly confirm, Channing's need for self-reliance was
always accompanied by an abiding fear of the autonomous self.
It is a perpetual paradox of his thought, indeed the central one,
that Channing is an individualist wary of the individual. The
problem of scripture was one more issue through which he had
to confront this quandary, because it forced him to abandon a
trust in the objective standard by which some men sought to
govern others. To a mind of classical temper, it was a trying
separation. Certainly for him, and perhaps for the whole New
England debate, the climax of the war between orthodoxy and
liberalism was Channing's shift from regarding truth as a sayable
thing to feeling it as a palpable thing.

As do many cruxes in the history of New England, the battle
over scripture reaffirms the wisdom of Perry Miller's pioneer
essay, "From Edwards to Emerson" (1940), for in returning to
the Edwardsean conviction that the final filter of truth must be
the individual perception, Channing simultaneously advanced
another step toward the Transcendentalist program.[52] He had
almost countenanced the internalization of the divine.

Channing's sense of the futility of verbal debate may have
begun as a conviction that fed on a pacific temperament, but it
ultimately become—if not in his hands—the basis for the Trans-
scendentalist renovation of language. "Historical Christianity,"

Emerson would declare, "has fallen into the error that corrupts all attempts to communicate religion."[53] Communication *is* the error. Long before Emerson spoke, Channing had taken a step toward abandoning the view of language as a communicative tool, toward construing it instead as a means of expression that, if sensitively used, allows the divine to speak through the self. As the Unitarian-Transcendentalist schism so often breaks down along lines of allegiance between Locke and Kant, so Channing may be regarded, in this context as in his conception of nature itself, as living in limbo. To understand him becomes once again a matter of withholding from the tag "transitional figure" its customary force of deprecation. Channing was not a fence sitter. He was a man possessed by doubt, and he had good reason to be.

Like his Transcendentalist heirs, he felt a disenchantment with language as it was currently constituted. Speaking long after the controversy over scripture, he warns a young minister, "There is danger that your mind may be frittered away by endless details, by listening continually to frivolous communication." The means of true human contact have transcended the verbal: "Every man is a volume, if you know how to read him. To seize the Universal in the particular, is the great art of wisdom, and this is especially important to one who is to live amidst details."[54] At his most natural, Channing displays an essentially classical mind oppressed by the bombardment of sound, images, events that have no coherence. Indeed the Baltimore sermon expresses a classicist's protest against deriving broad meaning from narrow premises, a resistance that Walter Jackson Bate has called central to the classical temperament: "To rest a determination of values upon the feelings, the floating inclinations, or the varying empirically-held opinions of particular individuality is to rest it upon the most fluid of foundations."[55] Channing finds that even the slavery crisis has its roots in a failure to discriminate justly between sensory messages: "He who cannot see a brother . . . under a skin darker than his own, wants the vision of a Christian. He worships the Outward." The same sensibility that allows Channing to ascribe slavery to a kind of naive symbolism ensures his disgust with the un-examined habits of the Boston elite, among whom his parishioners eagerly count themselves: "Another peculiarity of your ministry is, that you are to see human nature more undis-guised, naked . . . You are to go among those, who have not learned to cover up the deformities of the soul by courtesy and graceful speech."[56] Three decades after he earned the approval of Moses Stuart for not mincing words over sin, Channing's candor has not flagged. It is a curious myth that he regarded men through rosy spectacles, for neither the early nor the late stages of his career support such an inference. The middle years contain, at most, a dalliance with perfectionism. Slavery stopped the romance.

All around him, in racist politicians, in his genteel congre-gation, in the younger ministry, he heard wild abuse of lan-guage. Through it he saw moral confusion. In the case of the ministry the problem went hand in hand with a false academi-cism, a bookishness that Channing saw as the mark of a stale generation. His diagnosis was Emerson's: "Whilst you honor antiquity, you must remember that the past has not done and could not do the work of the present . . . Remember, too, that each man has his own way of working, and can work powerfully in no other, and do not anxiously and timidly model yourself after those whom you admire."[57] Edward Young's famous apho-rism provides an inescapable parallel: "He that imitates the *Iliad* is not imitating Homer." Like Young, Channing speaks from a classicism leavened by concern for man's continuing diginity and his continuing responsibility to himself.

Channing's alarm was not confined to a tired clergy. He speaks also of the prospects for liberty that culture, in the Arnol-dian sense of the word, can offer those in any social rank who open themselves to it: "Some seem to think that there is a kind of magic in a printed page, that types give a higher knowledge than can be gained from other sources. Reading is considered as the royal road to intellectual eminence [but] . . . Truly good books are more than mines to those who can understand them. They are the breathings of the great souls of past times. Genius is not embalmed in them, as is sometimes said, but *lives* in them perpetually."[58] Between those who skim a book in search of social polish and those who engage a living mind through its pages, Channing saw a widening distance. And all of these problems— the superficially educated, the dependent ministry, the manipulative politicians—became finally one problem. To meet it, or at least to address it, Channing undertook a campaign for the restoration of language to some semblance of integrity.

Scornful of a "blubber-lipt ministry," the first American Puritans had insisted that "writings that come abroad, they are not to dazzle, but to direct the apprehension."[59] Modernized in form, these words could be Channing's. Preaching in 1840 where Edwards had preached a century before, he prescribed what New Englanders had once known as the "plain style": "I exhort you first, to communicate the truth with all possible plainness and simplicity . . . Do not disguise or distort it, or overlay it with ornaments or false colors, to make it more effectual . . . Beware of ambiguous words, of cant, of vague abstractions, of newfangled phrases, of ingenious subtileties." This call for purification, for reducing language to its essentials, fills the late sermons: "the truth-preacher is free from all artifice and affectation of style and manner; . . . he is distinguished by simplicity, earnestness, naturalness, freedom . . . Without this, preaching is a tinkling cymbal, a vain show." The reaction against "the thirst for stimulants" is of course partly a recoil from the revivalism that intermittently swept the country during Channing's lifetime. "Everywhere people go to church to be excited rather than improved." But the ministerial office was misused by dullards as well as firebrands, and the slow-talking pedant was closer to home: "Let those who are to be educated here [in Harvard's Divinity Hall] be admonished against the frigid eloquence, the school-boy tone, the inanimate diction, too common in the pulpit . . . Let them . . . adopt the style and elocution of men who have an urgent work in hand, and who are thirsting for the regeneration of individuals and society."[60]

Since the days of the pamphlet war, Channing had been sensitive to the liberals' failure to stir excitement from the pulpit, and even his most lyrical sermon, the *Likeness to God* of 1828, concedes that he cannot "rival in sudden and outward effects what is wrought by the preachers of a low and terrifying theology."[61] One student of the period has made the interesting observation that the general shift in dominance from oratory to the printed word helps to explain the gentleness of Unitarian expression. For a reader to close a book upon an imprecatory passage requires less gumption than for a congregant to walk out in the middle of a sermon. A book has no eyes with which to follow; the page requires tact where the pulpit permits excoriation—and the temper of the written word inevitably affects the spoken.[62] Caught between colleagues sodden with literacy and a "low" evangelical clergy, with their "anxious bench" and the "falling, barking, catalepsy, rolling, running" that they inspired, Channing stood baffled—but there is no question that he finally preferred the risk of passion to the security of sloth: "Men will prefer even a fanaticism which is in earnest, to a pretended rationality which leaves untouched all the great springs of the soul, which never lays a quickening hand on our love and veneration, our awe and fear, our hope and joy."[63] As the scale swings toward meeting the need for homiletic power, Channing moves one more step in the transcendentalist direction. There is no denying that his own style sometimes falls into what Yvor Winters calls the "easy and well-constructed period, and . . . the highly generalized statement which tended at its best toward the aphorism, at its weakest toward the cliché."[64] But Channing shows a flair for rhythmic variation, for crescendo, and for a kind of congruence between sound and sense: "In peace, [Napoleon] delighted to hurry through his dominions; to multiply himself by his rapid movements; to gather at a glance the capacities of improvement which every important place possessed; to suggest plans which would startle by their originality and vastness; to project in an instant, works which a life could not accomplish." This parade of semicolons efficiently conveys the resistance to completion, the succession of provisional endings with which Napoleon punctuated his public life. By judicious anaphora, the essay excellently renders both the majesty and the petulance of its subject: "He was not to be measured . . . He was not to be retarded . . . He was not to be subjected." This trio begins a string of nine almost consecutive sentences that start with "he" or "his," nicely expressing the ego triumphant. And as his prose could rise to the challenge of Napoleon, so, in treating the temperamental divergence of Samuel Johnson from John Milton, it could find an equipoise satisfying without being soporific, relaxed without being flaccid. Channing presents the two figures as fell and mighty opposites; one casts light on "man's actual condition, on the realities of life, on the springs of human action," while the other speaks "not so much of what man is, as of what he might become."[65] The several pages of antithesis that he devotes to the opposition achieve a simultaneous balance and a straining apart that is worthy of the Johnsonian style itself. Indeed there are in Channing very close echoes of Johnson's phrasing, as when he speaks of "the insufficiency of worldly enjoyments," or remarks that "our wants, instead of being satisfied, grow with possession."[66]

Channing's own linguistic practice, then, by no means shuns rhetorical device; on the contrary, it reveals an almost instinctual urge to align the feel of the prose with the feel of the subject. This is a gift, in part developed consciously, but also utterly natural for a writer with an ear as good as Channing's. The question that it raises is whether he was easy in his craftsmanship, for there is no avoiding the fact that his is ultimately a manipulative technique. However tactful, it is a means of guiding the reader's, or hearer's, response. By participating in it—in art—Channing directly confronts within himself the problem of preaching for effect. And yet his constant counsel was "Exaggerate nothing for effect."[67] He practiced what he condemned.

The essential contribution of neoclassicism to the classical theory of mimesis has been succinctly stated by M. H. Abrams: "Art, it was commonly said, is an imitation—but an imitation which is only instrumental toward producing effects upon an audience."[68] This distinction helps to bring into focus the many ways in which Channing found himself hedged in by a utilitarian habit of mind. The rule of utility remained unsatisfying. As with all its forms—ethical, aesthetic, epistemological—utilitarianism destroys the hold of absolutes upon the imagination, weakens the barriers against relativism. We have seen Channing's alarm at that weakening, and we shall see more of it—but the point for now should serve as a reminder of his discomfort with what may be roughly called a neoclassical mentality. For Channing the pursuit of effect, without a firm grasp of the relation between man's passion and the stability of the divine, reflects a moral anarchism. It can degenerate into amusement, or worse, into the pleasure that one man derives from making another his puppet. Channing named it well: "By this sin fell the angels," he wrote at the end of his life, by this "lust for domination."[69]

What kept him from becoming just another half-hearted preacher is the fact that all these dangers, and all his hesitancy to endorse the primacy of feeling, were outweighed by another threat: "Do not speak as a machine, an echo, but from a living soul."[70] This warning always takes precedence. It is the key to

Channing's ministry because it is more affirmation than negation; it signals his flight from the paralysis around him. "A terror of living burial" is what one writer calls the dominant emotion of the liberal clergy,[71] and Channing felt that terror. Its reality most vividly appears in the discussion that took place within Unitarian circles over the virtues of preaching without notes: "The truth is," Henry Ware, Jr., admitted rather sadly, ". . . that it is not the weight of the thought, the profoundness of the argument . . . which interest and chain the attention of . . . those educated hearers . . . They are as likely to sleep through the whole . . . It is . . . the attraction of an earnest manner which arrests the attention."[72] Like the younger Ware, Channing approved of preaching without notes, but also like Ware, whose *Hints on Extemporaneous Preaching* (1824) falls into a tick-tock rhythm of suggestion and retraction, Channing wavers: "Every other sermon, I think, should be written, if circumstances allow it. But he who only preaches from notes, will never do justice to his own powers and feelings."[73] The spectacle of a ministry hunting for ways to keep its congregations awake is a disheartening one—but in the end Channing manages to retain his poise with an endorsement of extemporizing and a caution against theatrics.

The point that must not be missed amid this confused search for the right ministerial posture is that with all his various reluctance, Channing does join the search for effect, for power. Spurred by a sense of the liberals' imminent eclipse, he does cultivate in his own work what Ware calls "manner," and he sanctions it in others. His internal debate over the extent to which rhetorical flourish and techniques for popular appeal were justified may be seen as part of the larger accommodation by New England leaders to the techniques of electioneering that the Jeffersonians had introduced into American politics. Old-line Federalists were slowly awakening to the need for new gestures of respect toward the populace;[74] Channing too was fighting the extinction of his party by calling upon it to abandon its imperial posture. As we have seen, it was the release from scripture that first fixed his attention upon the need for linguistic reform. With time, he more and more insisted—perhaps for purposes of self-persuasion—that the corruption of language was the real culprit in the liberal-orthodox split, even in human animosity itself. He was willing to take chances for the sake of restoring the power of the word.

All of Channing's language reform hitherto described, some aimed toward achieving clarity, some toward energy, constitutes only a groundwork, not an actual beginning of the transcendental poetic. But there is a place in his work where he anticipates not only Emerson's diagnosis, but also Emerson's cure:

> It is objected to [Milton's] prose writings that the style is difficult and obscure, abounding in involutions, transpositions, and Latinisms; that his protracted sentences exhaust and weary the mind, and too often yield it no better recompense than confused and indistinct perceptions . . . We know that simplicity and perspicuity are important qualities of style; but there are vastly nobler and more important ones, such as energy and richness, and in these Milton is not surpassed. The best style is not that which puts the reader most easily and in the shortest time in possession of a writer's naked thoughts; but that which is the truest image of a great intellect . . . Its natural movement is free, bold, and majestic . . . A full mind will naturally overflow in long sentences, and in the moment of inspiration, when thick-coming thoughts and images crowd upon it, will often pour forth in a splendid confusion . . . We must not expect in the ocean the transparency of the calm, inland stream.[75]

These words remain those of an exhilarated observer rather than a participant; except in some breathless passages of *Likeness to God*, Channing did not reach the heights he celebrates. But critical sympathy is achievement enough. It is this receptivity to the public turmoil of Milton's prose that made the essay on Milton such a revelation to contemporary readers.[76] Channing had re-discovered a lost dimension of prose writing itself, the same treasure that Emerson and Thoreau would later fall upon: "If a man is inflamed and carried away by his thought . . . let me read his paper."[77] With more time and fewer restraints, they would augment it with works of their own.

Scholars sometimes have a weakness for the sentimental, a taste that readily inclines toward the image of a man longing for new worlds but crippled in his capacity to grasp them. It is not complete distortion to find such a man in Channing. But the fact that his own writing lacks what his criticism exalts is not ascribable only to a congenital, or socially caused, incapacity. Channing did see the glory in a prose that flowed from a deeper source than that department of the mind which handles messages. He did see the self-exploratory nature of literature, the abandon of a prose style that is truly an extension of the man. Awakened by Milton, his interest was further aroused through a little book by Rowland Hazard called *Language* (1836), a work that grants "that genius acts independently of general rules."[78] And so Channing sought to soothe Andrews Norton's outrage at the young Emerson's mystical chant; and so he ached for what Hazard called "the state of feeling which is produced by symphony."[79] He even looked with a touch of envy upon those who felt it.

It was not a late-life envy; there is already in this denial of 1815 an incensed tone reserved for accusations that hit home: "The publick feelings are . . . awakened against Unitarians . . . [by the claim] that they disbelieve the Trinity because the doctrine is mysterious and because they prefer reason to revelation, human wisdom to the wisdom of God."[80] Channing sensed what retrospect makes us feel today, that his orthodox opponents spoke from the heart, and with the purest motive, when they put aside the bickering and pleaded humility. This is Lewis Tappan on Christ's bound humanity and divinity: "I will cease, then, to be wise above what is written . . . The existence of these two facts is a mystery."[81] This simple concession is at once a plea that the liberals stop their whittling at God and that they grant mystery a reprieve. In listening to Hazard, in softening Norton's rage at Emerson and Ripley, Channing manifested a belated respect for Tappan's warning. Mystery was seeping out of the world, and those who might restore it were not to be lightly dismissed.

The yearning that underlies this tolerance is more than a passing mood. It is fully part of Channing, but it contends with his rationalism for his loyalty. Writing to Elizabeth Peabody after she sent him Theodore Parker's *Discourse on the Transient and Permanent in Christianity* (1841), he shows how well he knew himself and, near the end of his life, how honest he could be: "I owe the little which I am to the conscientiousness with which I have listened to objections springing up in my own mind to what I have inclined and sometimes thirsted to believe."[82] In that sentence lies much of Channing's greatness. The task of conveying that greatness today is largely one of juxtaposing the "objections" and the "thirst." The debate that Channing held with others and with himself on the place of scripture, and on the issues that flowed from its demotion, is a rich depository of both his longing and his restraint. He did anticipate the revolt against romanticism that later humanists like Irving Babbitt would lead, but he loved what he condemned.

In revising scripture in the light of reason, Channing had loosed a force that could not be selectively applied. What he sanctioned in the Baltimore sermon was the elevation, or at least the displacement, to the level of metaphor of those scriptural passages whose literal sense offended reason. Such a way of reading was not unknown in New England. As we have seen, Edwards practiced a form of it, and earlier still those Puritans who valued the law as man's best hope had hounded from the colony others who sought to "spiritualize" such Biblical commandments as the keeping of the sabbath "out of the world."[83] Indeed the peculiar consistency of Roger Williams had been to insist that if the Old Testament were to be read typologically, as a foreshadowing of the New, then its exemplary function must be dissolved. One could not choose some Jewish rules for keeping and others for throwing away. When they were told by Williams that their righteous sword was illegitimate, the magistrates simply wielded it and threw him into Rhode Island.

Channing did not share Williams's inexorable logic, but he faced the same problem, and his opponents told him so. Leonard Woods was quickest to point out the threat in liberal reading of scripture to the coercive power of law, but the immediate danger was to a different quarter, to the one article of faith that made plausible the liberals' claim to being Christians—their acceptance of the miracles as supernatural facts. "You may smile, my dear Sir," wrote Moses Stuart to Channing in 1819, "but I am entirely unable to see how [the explanations by German scholars of the miracles as natural phenomena] imply a greater liberty than you take with John 1:1, Rom 9:5, and many other passages."[84] Channing was not smiling. If Parker's *Transient and Permanent* (the bluntest antimiracle tract from within the Unitarian fold) unnerved him, charges like Stuart's had long before left his nerves raw, and others worried the wound: "The spirit of [the Unitarian] argument [against the Trinity]," wrote Samuel Miller, "is precisely the same with that of the celebrated infidel, Mr. *Hume*, against Miracles."[85] There are indications in Channing's work as early as the *Evidences of Revealed Religion* (1821) that such charges had taken effect on him, for he shifted, slightly but perceptibly, the basis of faith from the miracles themselves to the sincerity and passion of those who reported them.[86] It was a kind of appeasement.

What Channing's critics saw was that the technique of allegorizing the Bible would eventually undermine all scriptural function, including its celebration of the numinous. Channing himself—and this is the heart of his dilemma in the denominational wars—could see that the eradication of literal meaning in scripture would lead inevitably to a profusion of personal meanings. He had granted new license to the individual, so often the half-desired consequence of his reforms. This was not a novel theological problem, nor is its most obvious precedent Roger Williams. Augustine himself, in relocating the city of God in the soul, had found it necessary to allegorize the millennial predictions of *Revelation*, the same book that we have seen Edwards loosen from the literal.[87] To allegorize was to internalize, to bring the beatific (or the satanic) vision inside the mind, a move that Channing knew well: "Heaven," he wrote, "is a freed and sanctified mind"; and "Men are flying from an outward hell, when in truth they carry within them the hell which they should chiefly dread."[88] A learned scholar of romanticism has gone so far as to call this Augustinian impulse the seed of the romantic idea;[89] to internalize God's kingdom is to restore its meaning and to make the possibility of entrance into it a promise for every man, a work that art can further. To a mind possessed by the idea of an internal God, art no longer mimics heaven through its effect, it *becomes* heaven in its essence. Channing felt and aided this aesthetic and spiritual revelation, but he also felt the sorrow and reproach of those who huddled at Andover and Princeton, asking him whether this new order that he was helping to deliver would respect any of the old centers of authority, or whether it would make paradise for the self alone.

In a trenchant essay of forty years ago, Clarence Faust described how the orthodox took grim pleasure while the liberals cringed at the increasingly evident descent of transcendentalist conclusions from Unitarian premises.[90] Even in his lifetime, Channing was cast as the father of an infidel brood; he heard his paternity insinuated by those who called it disgrace and acclaimed by those who called it honor. One of his putative sons,

Theodore Parker, remembered him this way a week after he died: "It was a MORAL POWER that spoke in him . . . He saw through the shadows and into the reality of life. Many knew more of things as they are; few men have been so true to things as they ought to be."[91] Such a fidelity to human potential— which Channing had so gratefully found in Milton—is perhaps the most difficult value to transmit without confusing it with human ambition. Whether he finally passed it on to those whom everyone, foe and friend, called his spiritual children was an open question for him, as it remains for us.

4

Slavery and the Problem of Evil

LEDUC   I owe you the truth, Prince: you won't believe it now, but I wish you would think about it and what it means. I have never analyzed a gentile who did not have, somewhere hidden in his mind, a dislike if not a hatred for the Jews.

VON BERG   *clapping his ears shut, springing up*: That is impossible, it is not true of me!

LEDUC   *standing, coming to him, a wild pity in his voice*: Until you know it is true of you, you will destroy whatever truth can come of this atrocity. Part of knowing who we are is knowing we are not someone else. And Jew is only the name we give to that stranger, that agony we cannot feel, that death we look at like a cold abstraction. Each man has his Jew; it is the other. And the Jews have their Jews. And now, now above all, you must see that you have yours—the man whose death leaves you relieved that you are not him, despite your decency. And that is why there is nothing and will be nothing—until you face your own complicity with this . . . your own humanity.

—Arthur Miller

READERS OF *The Rape of the Lock* (1714) know that it exceeds the reach of satire, that under its delicacy there runs a terrible lament. The special mixture of rage and pity that constitutes the usual satiric voice achieves an elegiac dignity in the account of Belinda's world. Hers is a mental universe not unlike what Pope's dissenting contemporaries called the "damned estate," a world without clarity of vision, where lapdogs and husbands are equally mourned and nothing separates bibles from powder puffs, a world of living teapots and lifeless men. It is a plausible anteroom to hell.

And yet what makes it hellish is nothing active, nothing palpable. Lord Petre's villainy, for example, has more casual lewdness in it than obscenity; his soul is lost not through malice but because he is merely a shell. Pope's lifework—in his accommodation to Newton, in his zeal for correctness as the one way left of excelling—was to rise somehow above his fear of spiritual emptiness. The theme of privation is at the center of *The Rape*. The poem understands that men have lost their sense of sin, that they live in dread of the trivial hurt and in ignorance of the heroic:

> The Peer now spreads the glitt'ring *Forfex* wide,
> T'inclose the Lock; now joins it, to divide.
> Ev'n then, before the fatal Engine clos'd,
> A wretched Sylph too fondly interpos'd;
> Fate urg'd the Sheers, and cut the *Sylph* in twain,
> (But Airy Substance soon unites again)
> The meeting Points the sacred Hair dissever
> From the fair Head, for ever and for ever!
>
> (III, 147-154)

In a poem about absence (of mind as well as spirit—Belinda is always in a daze) the oxymoron of substantial nothingness is wickedly right. One of Pope's accomplishments is his consistent transformation of anxiety into verbal play, but the fun is never comforting, and the most somber business involves the man upon whom so many references converge, Milton, who stalks the poem like a disapproving father:

> The sword of *Satan* with steep force to smite
> Descending, and in half cut sheer, nor stay'd,
> But with swift wheel reverse, deep ent'ring shear'd
> All his right side; then *Satan* first knew pain,
> And writh'd him to and fro convolv'd; so sore
> The griding sword with discontinuous wound

Pass'd through him, but th'Ethereal substance clos'd
Not long divisible, and from the gash
A stream of Nectarous humor issuing flow'd
Sanguine, such as Celestial Spirits may bleed,
And all his Armor stain'd erewhile so bright.

(*Paradise Lost*, VI, 324-334)

To annotate the discrepancy between these lines and Pope's variation on them is to feel for a moment the shock that afflicted the poetic imagination as the Enlightenment extended its critique beyond superstition to religion itself. To applaud the triumph of reason without accepting the exile of God had become the critical challenge. Under that burden, Pope would have traded a kingdom of metric niceties for the grandeur of Milton's lines, and his wit is an effort to compensate for the loss. Satan could no longer "lift / Human imagination to such highth / Of God-like Power," because the devil, with God, was fading from Pope's culture. And so he was from Channing's.

To the English poet and the American clergyman the moral danger introduced by the death of Satan was much the same: a relativistic world trying to be born. But it must be remembered that Pope saw no means to recover Satan, while Channing did. Channing saw the chance where many American intellectuals saw it, in the specter of slavery—for slavery might sweep away the broken teacups, and botched dance steps, the silver scissors, and make the larger reality of evil inescapable even in a world of palaver. Men could not stay blind. "As our merchants and manufacturers cast their eyes Southward, what do they see? Cotton, Cotton, nothing but Cotton . . . Men call [slavery] in vague language an evil, just as they call religion a good; in both cases giving assent to a lifeless form of words, which they forget while they utter them, and which have no power over their lives."[1] But there was a chance for awakening. As Henry May has shown, rationalism had never quite captured the New World, but had always had to fight against a stubborn Calvinist heritage.[2] The

American imagination produced at best only awkward imitations of Augustan forms. Of course the literature of Channing's youth does look very much like its English models—the couplets of the Hartford wits, the epistolary novels, the gothic romance. If one stops with the outline, the literary histories of England and her colony do seem a double image, one displaced a little from the other in time. We see Edward Taylor preparing his "metaphysical" verses nearly a century after Donne, or Cotton Mather writing in the mode of Thomas Browne even as bundles of *The Spectator* were being unloaded on the Boston piers. This phenomenon still exercises Anglophile critics, but the issue of American derivativeness becomes interesting only with a closer look at the choices of emulation and at the nature of the copies. Timothy Dwight's *The Triumph of Infidelity* (1788), for example, though in the manner of Pope and Dryden, narrates a dramatic opposition quite incongruous with its structure; the shade of Dryden has no place here unless it is among the "subs" whom "Satan boasts . . . His Tolands, Tindals, Collinses, and Chubbs." Satan's "chief bane," his "apostolic foe," is inevitably Edwards, "that moral Newton . . . that second Paul," who "saw love attractive every system bind . . . Beneath his standard; lo what number rise, / To dare for truth, and combat for the skies!"[3] If these valiant couplets grow tiresome, it may be not only through technical deficiency but also because there is a built-in weakness in a literature that speaks antimodern sentiments through what its practitioners thought the most modern forms. Such incongruity of means and substance would be addressed in the several literary declarations of independence in the new century—by Bryant in the *Lectures on Poetry* (1825), Channing in his *Remarks on National Literature* (1830), Emerson in *The American Scholar* (1837). Similarly in the early American novel one finds a strained accommodation between content and form. Brockden Brown's Ormond, for example, is not so easily accounted for as Richardson's Lovelace, not so readily explained as an upperclass wretch feeding on his waiting-ladies. The social categories do not quite work, and so, in the hands of Brown, the rapist becomes something more sinister. Satan lived on in the New World.

Still, more than a century after Pope's protest that men had allowed the devil to die, Channing lamented the loss. But he felt it with a difference—a difference ensured by a provincial culture whose artists made portraits of that devil even while working in the most genteel forms. As Pope's *Essay on Criticism* (1711) seeks to versify rules (rules for writing and for living) and *The Dunciad* (1743) rails at those who love the rules while forgetting why they are needed, so did Channing's generation shudder to imagine what kind of art and what kind of life would emerge from an unregulated wilderness. But Channing is not another Pope, as Taylor was not another Donne and Mather not another Browne. And he is not for the same reasons. For if Satan lived in the poems (to Philip Freneau he was Cornwallis), and secretly through the stock figures of the novels, he lived more openly than ever—dragged into the light and held up for every man to see—in the sermons of those Americans who fought the Enlightenment tooth and nail. Channing felt their force. If Channing's response to evil is to make any historical sense, we must examine the truly indigenous American tradition that stretched behind him while not forgetting the rationalist alternative. Between the two is where Channing may be found. Though like Pope he paid homage to Milton, his essay on Milton formulates its lament in a distinctive American mode. To understand it one must look backward not only to the sylphs and gnomes but also to the Great Awakening. As the prelude to Channing's struggle with slavery, the Milton essay contemplates what an earlier New England minister had called "God's wisdom in the permission of sin."

Though speaking in an idiom foreign to Pope, the Calvinist

ministry in eighteenth-century America had contended with a periodic complacence not unlike the pretty tedium of *The Rape*. Jonathan Edwards himself filled his central work, *A Treatise on Religious Affections*, with outrage at the full-bellied contentment of New England's "formal hypocrites," a class in which the Lady Arabella Fermor would not have felt entirely out of place. Like Pope, Edwards sought to stop the drift toward a world where toiletries marked the fitness of a man for judgment; his hellfire sermons and *The Dunciad* are not such different enterprises as they might seem. The Americans had their own language for reacting to what we may roughly call middle-class values. To see just what middle ground Channing occupies between the two traditions, it is necessary to consider the subtle but crucial shift that American Protestantism underwent between Edwards's time and Channing's, especially as it dealt with the problem of sin.

In 1762, four years after Edwards died, one of his disciples, Joseph Bellamy, was appointed Election Preacher by the lower house of the Connecticut Assembly. In May he preached his Election Sermon. While speaking of the standing political order, he expressed a strangely eulogistic mood, but while prophesying, he celebrated "a whole society in perfect love and harmony," a society truer in spirit to the generous "civil privileges" with which the people of New England were blessed. Bellamy's words that day signaled the appropriation of Edwardsean ideas for political action. Love, as the saint's response to "beings and things as they are," was the force to be enlisted, and Bellamy's sermon, respectful though not deferential to the leaders of the moment, envisions an imminent shift from "civil rulers [with] . . . no . . . regard for the public weal," to a "governor [of] . . . good will and tenderness." In a nation on the edge of imperial crisis, Bellamy lived in keen anticipation of a time when God would test men's virtue. As evil multiplied, so would the Christian legions: "While our rulers and our teachers arm themselves against it, let every man in the colony join to stone it with stones, till it is dead—so let sin be slain."[4]

These predictions follow inevitably from Bellamy's conception of God's purpose in allowing sin in this world. Like his mentor, he conceived of history as ultimately—and imminently—progressive. Sin was a spur. The Jews, for instance, were made to suffer at Pharaoh's hands precisely that they might emerge ignited from the crucible. Lassitude was the devil's work; energy was God's. Bellamy's mind returns always to contemplate the actors in historical events. The thrust of his preaching penetrates to the individual heart, for that is where the divine work begins. He delights to catalogue each man's special contribution to the collective triumph: "Go to the clergy . . . to the merchant's shop . . . to the industrious farmer . . . to courts of justice . . . to the poor." His interest always revolves around one man's response to events, thus his way of imagining the millennium is to compose a series of soliloquies: like speakers in a miracle play, Paul, Adam, Gabriel, Moses, serially voice their ecstasy. The millennium for Bellamy is a massive inculcation of "holy joy" into the human heart.[5] God's majesty becomes almost an internal individual experience.

This psychological emphasis, so firmly in the Edwards tradition, constitutes the basis of theodicy: for Bellamy, God's final wisdom in permitting sin is illuminated by the fact that men are repaid for their suffering in tenfold gifts of joy. Their senses are heightened by trial. But such a reading of the historical role of sin did not long survive unaltered in the New England mind. Interestingly enough, it began to fail more or less concurrently with the war for independence. For while Bellamy's theodicy was an application of the doctrine of Edwards's great meditation *The End for which God Created the World*, not all of Edwards's children extended his principles with equal fervor. The most influential among them, and the one whom Channing knew best,

Samuel Hopkins, marked a shift into a minor key—and it is his legacy with which Channing found himself burdened.

In turning from Bellamy to Hopkins one notices first a loss of tautness in the style. This is a loosening, a drift toward generality that corresponds to a reduction of interest in the individual consciousness. Compare, for example, the openings of sermons by each on the providential role of sin. Bellamy begins sharply: "Jacob being dead and buried, and Joseph still governor over all the land of Egypt, his guilty brethren began to be afraid." This is Hopkins: "In this Psalm, God's care and protection of his church is celebrated . . . In the words now to be considered, the absolute and universal dominion of God . . . is asserted."[6] The passive, abstract constructions suggest that Hopkins's phrasing did not compensate for what Channing would later call his "untunable" voice. "Some of the tones," Channing remembered, "approached those of a cracked bell more nearly than any thing to which I can compare it."[7] But more than poor oratory, Hopkins's formulations display, both stylistically and thematically, a habit of deferral. As the listener had to endure prolix constructions from which the points emerge tardily, so did Hopkins set a tone that discouraged the excitement, the expectancy, that Bellamy stirred. The characteristic diffuseness of Hopkins's prose tends to drain away urgency. The millennium, approached through his labyrinths, becomes more a projected curiosity than a vivid hope. Hopkins has lost the rhythm of revival preaching.

Instead of mobilizing individual souls, this kind of preaching comes close to justifying passivity. Of course, Bellamy too had celebrated the overarching governance of God, but for him the deity actually found his personal completion in the intensity of human response. For Hopkins man becomes less a partner, more an onlooker. In a sermon of 1800—the year Channing returned to Newport and renewed his contact with him—Hopkins sketched a view of the utility of sin that is startling in its exclusion of man as historical agent: Though God obstructed Herod's will to murder Christ, he tolerated Pilate's surrender;[8] his action and inaction combined to allow the necessary first step toward human redemption, the tenure of Christ on earth. While this idea in itself is hardly heretical, Hopkins spares no means to impress upon his listeners a humbling sense of man's submission, a vision of God as puppeteer that leaves no room for human will. Indeed the will is variously assaulted in Hopkins's preaching until the Christian ideal becomes the annihilation not only of self-interest but of self-consciousness itself. Hopkins's delight flows from the cosmic plan, not from its impingement on the mind of man. The psychological dimension has been lost.

There are many manifestations of this shift in emphasis, not the least of which is Hopkins's lukewarm involvement with the millennium. At the bottom of his preference for abstraction and the cosmic perspective lies an animosity toward man; the prospect of judgment-day stirs him much more than does its blissful prelude. Bellamy, in his Edwardsean zeal for communion, had employed an ecstatic arithmetic to compute the higher and higher numbers of converted souls. Preferring a figurative reading of the Biblical "thousand-year" promise, he labored to construe its true duration as 360,000 years, a time "in which there might be millions saved, to one that has been lost."[9] For Hopkins, on the other hand, the shorter the better. He is eager for the end.

This kind of impatience stems from a deep skepticism toward human militancy. Man's assignment in the righteous war is announced almost parenthetically: "This battle . . . will not consist in . . . Christians raising armies, and fighting and carrying on war with the anti-Christian party . . . But it will be commenced and carried on by Christ . . . He will doubtless make use of instruments in the battle." Reluctant to acknowledge any human efficacy in God's plan, this is the voice of anxious Federalism. Napoleon and Paine inform its hesitancy; it is exactly the ethos from which Channing struggled to free himself. His life-long wariness of messianism has its foreshadowings here, as even the condescension of Christ must be discounted: "Jesus Christ [will not] come personally in the human nature from heaven to earth to reign."[10] These words issue from that corner of the Federalist mind in which the many eulogies on Washington were composed, for Washington's heroism lay supremely in his refusal to play the hero. "With grateful reverence," Channing later wrote, "we call Washington . . . the Father of his country, but not its Saviour . . . he was not a hero, in the common sense of the word."[11]

Hopkins's halting prophecies add up to something not quite premillenarian, but he has clearly moved Christ a good deal closer to the start of the eschatological process than where Bellamy had left him. Channing, as we have seen, was similarly inclined to think in terms of cataclysm rather than of slow progress toward the divine. Samuel Hopkins, with all his pious severity, had helped to extinguish the Edwardsean faith for Channing.

The key point to be drawn from this sketch of a disintegrating tradition is that its inheritors in the early years of the nineteenth century found themselves without any secure conception of "God's wisdom in the permission of sin." This, it may be objected, does more to liken Channing's generation to every other in human history than to distinguish it. But Channing was endowed by temperament, and by his place and time of living with a sense that New Englanders had once comprehended, or at least reconciled themselves to, the reality of evil. Of course the most common means of meeting the problem was the strategy that descended through Edwards's rationalist opponents, from Charles Chauncy to Andrews Norton, who taught the lesson that by banishing a lively sense of sin one could preclude the need to face it. Channing encountered that route through Hutcheson, and rejected it, but the real crisis would come when evasion of the issue became impossible, when the antislavery pleaders came knocking on his door. Before slavery became the insistent issue of his life—before the mid-1830s—Channing found himself exactly in the dilemma of Alexander Pope: facing a world beyond imprecation, where the imagination could no longer conjure Satan, where a vivid sense of the good was withering in the absence of its opposite. The heart of Channing's meaning is to be found in his effort to use the revival of evil, to tap the instincts of a country once more ringing with moral denunciation, in his search for retrieval of the good. He was, as ever, sensitive to the perils of self-deception in the effort. And so the abolitionists would come to hate him.

His effort begins with the Milton essay. Out of the evangelical context, the essay emerges as a call, like Bellamy's, made in a time of national self-congratulation, to recognize that human dignity resides in man's capacity to confront his bondage to sin. "That deep feeling of evils, which is necessary to effectual conflict with them, and which marks God's most powerful messengers to mankind, cannot breathe itself in soft and tender accents. The deeply moved soul will speak strongly, and ought to speak so as to move and shake nations." It should be noted that Channing wrote these words in the privacy of his study rather than speaking them from his pulpit. A few pages later he mixes an image of himself with that of Milton: "We delight to contemplate him in his retreat and last years."[12] This sentence signals his tentative solution, the idea of escape, which we have seen in several forms before. To understand the drama of Channing's later life is to see how the second sentence just quoted comes to seem to him a less and less adequate response to the first.

Implicit in the essay is a reading of *Paradise Lost* as a poem about a public man's return to private solace. This is not an eccentric fantasy of Channing's but a continually defensible read-

ing of the epic, and one suited to the critical temperament of its
time. It is worth noticing that in the year of its writing Channing
was in correspondence with William Roscoe, the ruined finan-
cier of Washington Irving's *Sketch Book*, a man whom bank-
ruptcy had isolated (like Milton, Roscoe lived in seclusion with
his daughters), a man whose "classic fountain . . . once had
welled its pure waters in a sacred shade,"[13] but did so no more.
Like Irving, Channing savored the sleepy wisdom of this disen-
franchised gentleman, and into this mold he sought to fit John
Milton. In fact this was the standard Milton of Federalist criticism. Joseph Stevens Buckminster, for example, could see that
Paradise Lost would never have been written if Cromwell's commonwealth had not collapsed (he speaks the same logic as Trumbull's M'Fingal), but he could not see that the poem was written
about that collapse.[14] One feels in reading the pages of the
Monthly Anthology that a classic is a book that every generation feels compelled to rewrite in its own image.

And so the ideal of Boston gentility transformed the works
it criticized. "It is the delight and charm of literature," wrote
Samuel Thacher in 1810, "that it affords us a refuge from the
tumults and contentions of active life—a spot, where we may escape from the hot and feverous atmosphere which we are compelled to breathe in the world, and enjoy that repose which we
find nowhere else; not always, alas! even in the holy walks of the
theological inquiry."[15] About those who left Arcadia for the
fray, like John Quincy Adams, who had once been Harvard's
Boylston Professor of Rhetoric and Oratory, the Boston literati
had no kind words. Adams returned the sentiment when Channing began his own repudiation of the studious ideal: "He
meddled," Adams sneered, "much with the subject of slavery."[16]
Slowly, even Buckminster felt the force of the public challenge:
"You who seek in learned seclusion that moral serenity, which is
the reward of virtuous resolution, remember you do not escape

from temptations, much less from responsibility, by returning to the repose and silence of your libraries."[17] Channing remembered this more and more clearly as the slavery crisis grew.

Still, Milton became a hermit for the first school of American critics, a temperamental cousin of George Washington, who had graciously retired to a squire's life at Mt. Vernon. For now the key point about Channing's essay on Milton is the wish embodied in its pages, pages that even include an appeal for gradualism in the abolition of slavery.[18] It is a wish to believe that the inward turn is morally sufficient, the same turn that Channing had taken from nature and from history. It is far more a hope than a conviction, and Channing will soon abandon it.

In the years following his endorsement of the "paradise within," Channing began to be visited by abolitionist leaders. They came to ask for help. Their reports of their reception are not flattering to Channing. Edward Abdy, an English caller of ample indignation, recounts that Dr. Channing was unable to distinguish between indictments of American racial attitudes and attacks on his personal demeanor toward blacks. When the republic was accused, he defended himself. To Abdy, Channing was simply attempting "to find in the extent and intensity of a prejudice a reason for its continuance." Lydia Child credited him with even less, finding him possessed by a "characteristic timidity," a man who "carried his cloak on his arm for fear of changes in temperature," who in the next world would appear "in velvet slippers, on the softest carpet."[19] He was not, alas, the right commandant for Mrs. Child's battalion. The model of reclusive Milton still obtained.

But behind the eager slanders one can discern a somewhat different figure, a prickly man whose recalcitrance has another dimension than those its victims allowed. James Birney, for example, by 1836 was writing of Channing with large respect; one year later he would propose him as head of a new antislavery party.[20] "Velvet slippers" was neither new nor conclusive; the fabric and garment changed, but all his life Channing was berated for a womanish guise. The one thrust of the attack that does merit a pause is Abdy's observation of Channing's refusal to distinguish between affronts to the nation and to himself. This is a real clue to the psychological impact of the slavery crisis, for Channing's polemics make up a record of the narrowing gap between his self-image and his idea of America herself. His great trouble with the abolitionists was with their sundering the country into halves of virtue and vice, their imputation of purity to themselves. He was balking, once again, at the externalization of sin.

The abolitionist thunderings of the 1830s, most conspicuously those of William Lloyd Garrison, are extraordinarily defensive documents. And their defensiveness nurtures self-involvement; Garrison's landmark *Thoughts on African Colonization* (1832) is perhaps the best example of his captivity to the need for self-defense. Its early pages ramble through a series of declamations on the virtues of the cause, leaving the reader with the feeling that near the heart of the debate lies motive, intent, as much as the condition of Negroes. Under attack, Garrison grew unctuous: "I NEVER WILL DESERT THE CAUSE. In my task it is impossible to tire: it fills my mind with complacency and peace. At night I lie down with composure, and rise to it in the morning with alacrity. I NEVER WILL DESIST FROM THIS BLESSED WORK."[21] Before the 1960s historians were generally hard on the Garrisonians, taking them to task for just such an inclination to self-advertisement, even extending the indictment to the whole antislavery crusade. "An elite without function," is one historian's phrase,[22] and the note of social insecurity does sound through the *Thoughts*, betraying a certain grasping after social purpose through the device of outrage. But the same historians who pioneered the lowering of Garrison's stock simultaneously raised that of Theodore Weld.[23] The organized moderate versus the

firebrand anarchist has always been a historical schema of intrinsic appeal. Yet even in Weld there runs a theme of authorial
virtue, in his case more by negation of the enemy than by affirmation of the self. One suspects that his *American Slavery As It
Is* (1839) still irks, even instigates, those statisticians who have
recently tried to soften the image of the "peculiar institution."

The historians' retrospective chastisement of the abolitionist
leaders is an echo of the original debate, a debate in which Channing's voice underwent complex change. The first phase remains
in conformity to the isolated ideal of the Milton essay. "The
Abolitionists have done wrong," he writes in 1836, "they have
fallen into the common error of enthusiasts, that of taking too
narrow views, of feeling as if no evil existed but that which they
opposed."[24] Acquittal of the self is the habit Channing chafed at
when Abdy and Mrs. Child came visiting. It is an indulgence he
always would reject, but as he heard the rising pitch of national
anguish he rested less easily in the sanctuary of political isolation. Representatives of every antislavery faction sought an
audience with him. Even with his "velvet slippers" he was a
coveted prize.

And still he resisted: "The energy of will . . . ought to
regard the whole, in its strenuous efforts for a part." But slowly
there appeared in Channing's tone a concession that staying
above the fray carried its own moral pitfalls; for while he balked
at the self-involvement of the crusaders, he himself
pleaded—more abstractly, but still unambiguously—in favor of
the very exploitation he deplored: "We ought to think much
more of walking in the right path than of reaching our end. We
should desire virtue more than success . . . the first object of a
true zeal is not that we may prosper, but that we may do right,
that we may keep ourselves unspotted from every evil thought,
word, and deed."[25] The tangled rhetoric of these sentences constitutes a reminder of the moral confusion left by the shift from
Bellamy's activism to Hopkins's passivity. For Channing is

employing here the very language of Edwards's highest principle, the ideal of self-transcendence. "The first objective ground
of gracious affections," Edwards had preached, "is the tran-
scendently excellent and amiable nature of divine things, as they
are in themselves, and not any conceived relation they bear to
self, or self-interest."[26] Channing's "it is not that we may
prosper" echoes that cardinal tenet. But veiling this idea is the
exactly contrary notion that the moral safety of the self super-
sedes one's obligation to the other.

The tension so graphically illustrated by the proximity of
these conflicting phrases is one in which Channing could not
long exist. He knew that innocence can be a kind of self-interest,
and yet he could protest that "the first question to be proposed
by a rational being is not what is profitable, but what is Right"
and that "all prosperity, not founded on [the right], is built on
sand."[27] In the middle 1830s, then, he found himself denouncing
the subjective morality of the abolitionists while participating in
it himself. In the summer of 1834 one of his visitors, Samuel
May, said as much.[28] Channing, shaken, grew angry with himself.

It took years for the anger to show. The letter to Jonathan
Phillips, which Channing composed in 1839 in response to
Henry Clay's attacks on abolitionist tactics, marks a turning
point on the road to political commitment. It contains, first of
all, a growing recognition of Northern complicity: "The Free
States are the guardians, and essential supports of slavery. We
are the jailors and constables of the institution." Three years
earlier he had confidently declared, "no power but that of the
slaveholding states can remove the evil." The intervening time
had seen a redistribution of responsibility in his mind, a process
pressed forward largely by the early fugitive slave laws. He
could no longer say "[The South] alone can determine and apply
the true and sure means of emancipation . . . not that I think of
drawing up a plan; for . . . no individual so distant can."[29] The

coercion to sin, the pressure of intolerable law—these were the realities of the young republic, and they marked the beginnings of Channing's transformation from a man who would, at almost any cost, defend the standing order against subversion to a man whose deepest instincts pushed him toward rebellion. Over the problem of law Channing began to fight an internal civil war that would last as long as he lived.

In her jibe that he fretted over the weather report, Mrs. Child was groping for a true psychological insight: Channing *was* internally divided almost to a point of paralysis, though the question before which he truly froze was not the choice of over-coat but his relation to institutions. All his life he valued prece-dent, and when the South's apologists appealed to institutional continuity they spoke straight to his nerves. And yet he hounded them for their ploy: "As if an evil lost its deformity by becoming an institution . . . its being so rooted . . . [is] the very reason for vigorous opposition."[30] Channing had tried, unsuccessfully, to avoid that conclusion. Here, one year after Emerson's *Divinity School Address*, he conceded the practical inevitability of Emer-son's anti-institutionalism.[31] He could no longer evade the fact that tradition in America—what little there was of it—had become a salve for hypocrisy.

Though its participants called him serene in the eye of their storm, the slavery debate became a varied subversion of Chan-ning's most basic assumptions. By 1839 he understood where the most ominous challenge would strike: he was losing his trust in law. We have seen that since childhood he had felt uncomfort-able in the presence of its practitioners, in the places consecrated to its enforcement. Now his suspicions exploded, for law was the great shield of slavery. It spoke the unspeakable; it called mad-ness sane. It said that Garrison was a ranter and Henry Clay a citizen. For Channing the turn into the 1840s, the last thirty months of his life, was an embarkation into loneliness. Nature, history, scripture, had fallen—now law.

The law was shedding its pretence of virtue, asking finally that men embrace it because it was all they had, all they had to keep from savaging each other. In 1839 the process had only begun; its crescendo came for Channing two years later in his response to the case of the *Creole*, a slave ship seized and diverted to British Bermuda by the slaves it carried. The magnificent essay *The Duty of the Free States*, which would be in many ways his masterpiece, is adumbrated in the smaller, more personal memorial sermon for Charles Follen.

The Follen sermon is both an essay toward theodicy and a farewell to a dear friend. The German-born minister, one of the key conduits of "transcendental" thought to New England, had died in January 1840 on the burning deck of the steamship *Lexington* en route to dedicate his new church, a position that Channing had helped him secure. It had been a difficult task to settle Follen with any congregation, as he had acquired the reputation as something of a troublemaker. Associated with Garrison's *Liberator*, and proud of it, Follen refused to separate his religion from his politics. His death—not at sea, but in an inland waterway—carried for Channing the fullest measure of tragedy. As we know from Dickens through *David Copperfield* and from Melville through *The Encantadas*, the foundering ship close to shore struck the mid-century imagination with a special force, perhaps because it so cruelly witnessed the illusory nature of man's competence to control his destiny. For Channing, Follen's death was such a reminder of the most personal sort.

The first moments of his eulogy are an exquisite confession that Follen's commitment had become, through his death, a chastisement of Channing's aloofness. "Sometimes the religious man, with good intentions, but wanting wisdom and strength, tries to palliate the evils of life, to cover its dark features, to exaggerate its transient pleasures."[32] Few things in public oratory are more chastening or freer from bombast than this kind of private apology to an absent friend. It is the kind of speech that leaves an audience feeling they have missed something they were meant to miss, but it penetrates nevertheless to the heart. Channing in the last months of his life achieved a new self-critical candor: "My tendency," he confided to Mrs. Child six months before he died, "is to turn away from the contemplation of evils."[33] Follen's death has made him ashamed.

But the power of the sermon does not flow from secret confession. It is more than the expression of personal grief because it attempts to sketch a theodicy. In the attempt it leaps backward over a century to a world view closer in spirit to Bellamy than to Channing's contemporaries. For in the Follen sermon Channing explicitly rejects the notion of man's attenuated vision, the idea so often appealed to by the romantic mind in its struggle to palliate suffering.[34] This, for example, is Friedrich Schleiermacher: "The world is a work of which you see only a part . . . If a loftier unity is to be suspected, along with the general tendency to order and harmony, there must be here and there situations not fully explicable."[35] This is exactly the recourse that Channing admits to having preferred and vows to follow no more. He now considers it an evasion because it condescends to man. Paradoxically, in view of his provisional assent to romanticism, Channing insists that man *can* know his lot, can comprehend and accept his predicament. It is paradoxical because with all their exaltation of the human mind, the high romantics sometimes cannot fully grant this capacity. The majesty of Channing's rationalism is its willingness to treat the mind with this ultimate respect.

The key to the resolution, which harks back to Bellamy's brand of piety, is the insistence that pain turns the human mind toward God, that "there is a higher good than enjoyment; and this requires suffering in order to be gained." A man discovers himself in suffering. He is amazed that there exists a dimension to his life beyond the reach of the physical. The spirit is revealed when the body fails. The vision here recalls a time-honored comfort to which American thinkers often turned in periods of spiritual deadness; it is really the same discovery that Cotton Mather set forth with joy in *The Wonders of the Invisible World* (1693), the vision, in Channing's words, that "good and evil are never disjoined," that the ascendancy of blackness turns the mind to God. "The mind of Massachusetts," George Bancroft wrote at nearly the same time that Channing eulogized Follen, "was . . . more ready to receive every tale from the invisible world, than to gaze on the universe without acknowledging an Infinite Intelligence."[36] "Every tale" meant every tragedy as well as every romance, and though Bancroft was writing of the psychological need that had sown the witchcraft hysteria one hundred fifty years before, the habit that he identified was a persistent one. God, even to the least miracle-minded of New England Unitarians, still spoke through catastrophe as well as through blessing. Satan remained God's agent.

This faith obliterates the Hopkinsian variant on Edwards, for it refuses the image of man as a passive creature whose highest goal must be to submit to manipulation. It insists, on the contrary, that man's internal turmoil is the gift of God, that God lives in the human soul, and that man's goal is the transformation of this indwelling principle into energy. In making this point the Follen sermon achieves a synthesis between theology and poetic lament; it not only celebrates Follen as a godly man of action but shows that godliness *must* be active. It is a significant work of American literature because it grants a rare glimpse of a substantial thinker at the moment when he changes the course of his life. Gentle as it is, it is Channing's declaration that he will live differently in the time that remains to him. The old unity of piety and action is reconstituted in its pages.

In the spring following Follen's death, Channing journeyed to Northampton to preach the ordination sermon for John

Sullivan Dwight, a descendant of Jonathan Edwards. Dwight's ancestor looms over the sermon rather like Milton over *The Rape of the Lock*. The ministry, Channing warns, has lost its stability by losing its spine, and in his elaboration one hears not only the grumbling of his Federal Street parishioners but also the resentment of an earlier Northampton at a minister who insisted on restricting communion: "Wait not to be backed by numbers . . . Wait not till you are sure of an echo from a crowd." Preaching in the town that harried Edwards from his pulpit and endured his scorching farewell, Channing speaks with acute awareness of where he is standing: Edwards's name, he says simply, "has shed a consecration over this place." More than conventionally respectful, the sermon is also Edwardsean in theme: "Preach not with selfish regards . . . but with . . . disinterest, over-growing love."[37] In the aftermath of Follen's death, and amid the rising rancor of the slavery debate, Channing has become obsessed with the issue of selfishness. The ordination sermon for Dwight is a telltale product of the period between the death of Follen and the composition of *The Duty of the Free States*. It was an interval of trial.

No one can possibly read the later Channing as a romantic optimist. Channing's sensitivity to human depravity has not diminished, it has grown: "It is the existence of [a] mighty antagonist force to virtue in human nature," he declares in 1840, "which makes Christianity necessary."[38] If his earlier thought had construed the religious impulse as an urge toward elevation, he comes in his later years to feel it much more as a combat. The central importance of the slavery issue is that it identifies two enemies: the defenders of slavery, and the self.

What Channing tried to do, at the cost of his prestige among the abolitionists, was to assault one of these enemies without losing sight of the other. It was a fight carried on with divided resources, and there is a special strain in the knowledge that the old friend of last resort—the self—has revealed itself as an untrustworthy ally, even a foe. The Follen funeral sermon had articulated the old idea that evil exercises virtue—Mather's idea, and Bellamy's—an idea on which Channing's contemporaries proposed to act, and to act immediately. As one historian puts it, they had found in slavery a "satanic showcase,"[39] and in announcing their discovery some, like Garrison, could sound as much like self-therapists as had Cotton Mather in 1693. This self-concern made Channing cringe. The problem of distinguishing motives of militancy was an old one—time has hardly exhausted it—but the politics of Channing's era had renewed the difficulty to an unprecedented intensity. Zeal for reform, Channing knew, is "often forced, got up for effect, a product of calculation, not a swell of the heart."[40]

To read the history of reform is to see an ancient connection between self-involvement and selfless action. Among the earliest of Channing's models for rectitude on the slavery question, Samuel Hopkins himself had allowed an insidious conflation of external sin with the evil on his doorstep. In 1776, of all years, Hopkins had raged that the slave trade was corrupting the Africans *in Africa*, turning them into informers and what we now call quislings, cleaving them into sections. Under the pressure of the white man's greed, the coast-dwellers bartered the freedom of the inland natives for trinkets and for bits of gold. But the further one reads into Hopkins's tract—a tract Channing very likely heard or read in some form—the more one feels that his text could have served equally well as a diatribe against colonial dissension on the American continent. It is, with a few changes of detail, an acceptable account of the divisive impact of the war for independence. Informed by the first hand experience of an author who watched Tories and Whigs burn each other's houses, it builds more than an unconscious parallel between the continents. For Hopkins comes to argue quite explicitly that the evils of the slave trade, so devastating in

Africa, were coming home to haunt the customers. When he shifts into an attack on the business in rum, Newport's staple, the transition is almost imperceptible.[41] Thus, sixty-five years before Channing raised the issue in Northampton, the emancipation of Negro slaves and the tranquillity of the society they were meant to serve had become essentially the same issue. We have long recognized that the advocates of slavery argued that Negro freedom would threaten the white man's world; what has been less obvious is the utilization by the antislavery party of the same fear of disorder. Self-interest, from the start, was indivisible from abolition.

Long before Hopkins—at least as early as Samuel Sewall's *The Selling of Joseph* (1700)—slavery had fueled that especially American form of oratory, the jeremiad. It provided a foreign enemy whose strength could be used as an inverse measure of the health of New England. The idea of war as self-therapy, as Richard Slotkin has recently shown,[42] began early in America. The habit grew. Indeed the affinity between opposition to slavery and an aggressive defense of New England's cultural unity manifests itself in the first mature expressions of literary regionalism. The development from *Uncle Tom's Cabin* (1852) to *Oldtown Folks* (1869), for example, epitomizes the connection. Harriet Beecher Stowe, who eulogized Hopkins in fiction and whose father had been one of the last to try to hold together the national and regional antislavery programs,[43] sacrifices between those books the antisentimentalism, the necessary irony, that elevates *Uncle Tom's Cabin* to the stature of art. The smug, racist condescension of Miss Ophelia, whose moral inadequacy is the saving insight of that book, largely fades away in *Oldtown Folks*, giving way to a precious local virtue. Stowe's imaginative retreat into a closed domestic circle is a logical extension of the fear that lies at the heart of *Uncle Tom's Cabin*, and which Hopkins portends. In a justly famous sentence, Leslie Fiedler has struck to the heart of the matter, not

only for Stowe but for the whole period, for the apologists as
well as the abolitionists: "The chief pleasures of *Uncle Tom's
Cabin* are . . . rooted not in the moral indignation of the
reformer but in the more devious titillations of the sadist."[44]
Fiedler's formulation of the defensive hostility in the New
England mind, its relish at the spectacle of Christian submission
to torture, must be adjusted after *Uncle Tom's Cabin* to include
the New Englanders' capacity for willful evasion, since Stowe's
response in *Oldtown Folks* to the coming vengeance of the
enslaved (and to that which had already come in four years of
civil war) is to exile such untidiness utterly from the purview of
the novel. In *Uncle Tom's Cabin* the strategy had been to
emasculate the Negroes. Stowe's triumph lay in her rendering of
Tom as an incarnation of the suffering servant and the
conversion of fiery Mas'r George into a docile family man.
George moves from preaching revolt to preaching emigration;
Mrs. Stowe can conceive of free blacks in Liberia but not in
Mississippi. The degeneration from those elements of *Uncle
Tom's Cabin* that retain their power to frighten, from a world in
which it is possible for "property [to] get into an improper state
of mind," to the self-congratulatory idyll of *Oldtown Folks* is
precisely the descent that Channing foresaw and sought to avert.
"The great revelation which man now needs is a revelation of
man to himself."[45]

Mrs. Stowe was a specific realization of an intellectual
tendency that Channing knew in the abstract. To demonstrate
fully his dilemma, one must notice not only the clerical leaders
who preceded him, nor only the psychology of charity that
followed him, but the men with whom he sat and talked and
argued in the years of decision. John Greenleaf Whittier, who
has been proposed for decades as a direct influence on
Channing's antislavery opinions,[46] participated in the commerce
between regional pride and abolitionist indignation. *Snow-
Bound* (1866), the representative poem of post-Civil War New

England, is a work of retrospective celebration, an outpouring of nostalgia for a violated insularity: "Shut in from all the world without, We sat the clean-winged hearth about, / Content to let the north-wind roar" (ll. 155-157). The verse adores maternal Massachusetts, tells "the story of her early days" (l. 226), and makes explicit the linkage between New England household virtues and the eventual extinction of slavery, the Southern sin. (ll. 216-233). A full twenty years before this poem was written, when Whittier's point of view was alarmed and prophetic rather than sad and retrospective, he brought to his analysis of the slavery issue the same assumptions upon which he would build *Snow-Bound*: "[Slavery] crept into the Commonwealth like other evils and vices." An invasion by an alien culture, the fugitive slave bills undermined the "time-honored defences of personal freedom [and] the good old safeguards of Saxon liberty."[47] Like the sturdy parents who had battened down the hatches against snow and hail, the "brave old generation" that had kept out the slave-contaminant now "passed away"—a generation whose ancestry the sons must labor to deserve.

From these sons—Channing's colleague in the Federal Street pulpit among them—there came increasingly uncertain guidance. Twelve years after Channing's death, Ezra Stiles Gannett stood in his church and, like Whittier and Stowe and Hopkins, conflated the issues of opposition to slavery and Northern unity. By now that unity had become terribly fragile, "We stand in special need of calm and resolute minds . . . we can explain men's opposite behavior, without imputing to them bad hearts."[48] This is what the New England pride had come to, a conciliatory appeal for calm. More than ever, the orderliness of his own house was the New Englander's first concern.

Still, deliberate candor about the primacy of that concern requires a greater self-consciousness than Whittier, Stowe, or Gannett possessed. Henry Thoreau had it in abundance. His is the frankest and simplest link between the abolitionist impulse and a zeal for self-definition: "How many a man," Thoreau writes in his *A Plea for John Brown* (1859), "who was lately contemplating suicide has now something to live for!"[49] The *Plea* may stand as the capstone of its lineage, for though it transforms community pride into personal defense, the two instincts revolve around the same center.

Perhaps the most devastating critique of the Northern reform impulse in all its varied forms is to be found not in the revisionist historians of abolition, but in the work of the novelist who coined the phrase "the New England conscience." *The Bostonians* (1886) anticipates Fiedler's attack with a fierceness that borders on misogyny. James's heroine practices a "fraud upon her own imagination," drifts in tow to a stern spinster who "suffered less than she had hoped," who in turn follows a veteran of the feminist wars who in her young years "was in love only with causes, and . . . languished only for emancipation. But they had been the happiest days, for when causes were embodied in foreigners (what else were the Africans?), they were certainly more appealing." Olive Chancellor, the middle term of the trio, "quivers when she describes what [her] sex had been through," and sways between masochism and a vicarious sexual life achieved through her beautiful disciple. The whole sewing circle collapses when an oily Southerner who likes "the zest of forcing an entrance," enters their "cottage-fortress" and brings the young beauty "out to him . . . quite limp and pale from the tussle."[50] It takes only one Mississippian to vanquish three New England ladies. By comparison, Mrs. Stowe comes through Fiedler's barrage unscathed.

Without the license of hindsight, Channing was less hard on his enemies than either James or Fiedler, but their retrospective ridicule would not have shocked him. Before his eyes his contemporaries were fusing into one emotion the hatred of slavery and the self-love implicit in the love of New England. Channing understood this partnership before it was sealed, and the more deeply he penetrated it, the less violently he attacked the Southern slaveholder. It was this diminishing fury that disgusted some of his peers. But at the same time as he grew quieter, he came closer to active abolitionism. This is the paradox that must be understood in order to place him in the antislavery movement. As the Dwight ordination sermon confirms, his pride steadily slackened from *Slavery* in 1836 to the Jonathan Phillips letter of 1839 to the majestic Follen sermon of 1840, and as his self-satisfaction waned, his political engagement grew. He is a key figure of his time because he grasped the moral perils of political commitment and only then committed himself to politics. He teaches here the same lesson as in his struggle toward enlistment in the romantic movement; the fullness of his comprehension of the nature of both courtships makes his moments of assent genuinely moving.

The culminating document of these years, perhaps of Channing's life, is *The Duty of the Free States* (1842). When news of the *Creole* mutiny reached him, Channing understood immediately that the American demand for return of the criminal slaves—put forth by Secretary of State Webster— devolved into a general claim for deference by all nations to American law. In rejecting both the specific request and the general principle, Channing now moved, fully aware of what he was doing, into insubordination. He also guaranteed the outrage of those whom he had displeased with the Follen sermon. Some months later he would complete the break in eulogizing another friend, the reformer Joseph Tuckerman: "We hope to keep our little circle pure amidst general impurity. This is like striving to keep our particular houses healthy, when infection is raging around us."[51] Now, with his bridges burnt, Channing insists that the rights of man cannot be restricted by the state because they are not given by the state. Slavehood is a legal imposition with absolutely no intrinsic sanction, for total separation exists between the condition of being a slave and that of being a man. The advent of this division in Channing's thought has its significance not in the idea itself but in the conscious reversal to which he subjects its implications, a reversal of his own previous use of the distinction. In the lectures on "self-culture" (1838) he had employed exactly the same idea for the purpose of espousing a spiritual liberation within—but without affecting the outward condition of—a man's worldly estate. A man can be free in chains, he had taught in the 1830s; he had preached passivity to the poor by teaching the illusory nature of poverty; in fact the sermons on poverty had become disquisitions on the non-material harmony of the universe.[52] As David Brion Davis has shown, this kind of division has always lain at the heart of Christian apologetics for social inequality and for slavery itself.[53] Manumission, for example, could be urged by medieval Christians as human emulation of man's deliverance by God from sin, but it could also be resisted by appeal to the fundamental Augustinian distinction between this world and the world of the spirit. In *The Duty of the Free States* Channing refuses to rest any longer in this pious conservatism, and by refusing he reverses the direction of his own social thought. His embrace of abolition signals a new conviction that these divided and distinguished worlds must be joined. In his last years he fights for their conjunction.

The Duty of the Free States makes Channing's clearest declaration of a return from Hopkins to Bellamy. Channing was fed up with the idea of passivity in others and with the feeling of it in himself. "Evil," he had long before insisted, "is permitted by the Creator, that we should strive against it." Now he acted on that belief. *The Free States* is an incendiary document, a call, directed both outward and inward, to rise from sluggishness; in its own way it recaptures the rhythm of revival preaching that Hopkins had lost. In this sense it may be seen as a complementary document to the works of those revivalists whose spirit is generally described as anathema to Channing. Indeed it is too often forgotten that Channing himself carried on the revivalist tradition, that he sought "to persuade the sinner, by a salutary terror, to return to God."[54] Charles Grandison Finney, the "high priest of the Great Revival," shared Channing's sensitivity to the moral challenge of abolition. More like Channing than any Boston liberal, Finney denounced "the anti-slavery impulse . . . when it ceased to be a missionary movement to save the slaveholders . . . from [what Finney called] 'their state of desperation,' and became a drive for petitions to support a sectional war."[55] In 1837 he preached in New York on "self deceivers": "[You who] are hearers of the word but not doers . . . I say to you that YOU DECEIVE YOURSELVES."[56] Channing, as we have seen, was making the same homily to himself. And so with repeated thrusts, The Free States assaults the Hopkinsian vision of the individual's passive absorption into a larger whole.

Among the essay's sharpest insights is that the "annihilation of the individual by merging him in the state lies at the foundation of despotism." That the isolation of an oppressed minority is the inevitable accomplice, indeed the underside, of passionate nationalism is a lesson our own century has amply confirmed. What Channing saw amid the recrimination and invective of the North-South dispute was the simple fact that if the law could make a slave it could make anything. Vileness was no bar to its authority. The law, therefore, comes under attack in The Free States as nothing else had ever been attacked by Channing—not the trinity, not the Calvinists, not the Jacobins. " 'The voyage was perfectly lawful,' we are told,"[57] and he repeats the phrase, allowing it to fall into a singsong cadence, a litany like that of a child who delights in making a word sound absurd by repeating it till the vowels and consonants run together into babble. It is a grim pleasure, as "lawful" becomes a profanity through his pages, and the uglier it sounds the smaller an avenue of escape Channing leaves himself. This is the closest thing in his work—and it is closer in its political implications than anything in Emerson—to a truly antinomian utterance. It is an outburst of disgust at the audacity with which man dares to codify his barbarism by expressing it in rules.

In consequence of this revulsion, *The Free States* turns, but only briefly, to nature for reprieve. "No state can write its laws on that restless surface [of the sea]." But the effort is half-hearted to hold back the pollutant of civilized forms, because *The Free States* cannot finally posit a natural immunity to sin or even a gap between nature and man. Channing has come far beyond a notion of sin as a removable layer. He feels it now as the Puritans had felt it, as an invasive thing, a thing intertwined with virtue—within, not upon the soul. Though the essay certainly does imagine a better kind of law than that which governed mid-century America, it is not a reform proposal, not a call to rewrite wrong-headed legislation. More a secessionist document, it ultimately speaks something closer to the language of Calhoun than that of Webster, almost conceding the impossibility of just union. "America," it maintains, "is a league of sovereignties."[58] In this way Channing's late political utterances constitute a return to the days of the Hartford Convention, but with the great difference that under the whispered idea of disunion there now lies the long labor of his ministry, his ceaseless exploration of the power of self-interest in human affairs. The Channing of 1842 does not stand with the Channing of 1812. The Milton essay in its exploration of retreat had mediated between the two, and the sobering insight that came upon the aging Channing was that virtue resided neither in the united nation nor in any fragment—region, state, or self. What *The Free States* says is that there can be no rest either in authority or in individual dissent, that man is condemned to ceaseless struggle between the two. With death not far from him, Channing embarked on that struggle.

It was a very lonely time. His world, the world of Mount Vernon Street and Louisburg Square, was furious at him for his failure to defend the commercial network it called its nation. The world of Garrison and Child was through with him for his failure to recognize the righteous new nation they had founded. Channing shared this limbo with the best minds of his time, but loneliness can be a thing unmitigated by sharing.

The Duty of the Free States should be read as one among those mid-century expressions of alarm, even despair, at the unsatisfying choice that America now offered between a cheapened communitarian ideal and the grandiose self. It joins the company of the Leatherstocking novels (1823-40), *The Scarlet Letter* (1850), and *Pierre* (1852), a book in which Melville too has words for the law: "In the cold courts of justice the dull head demands oaths and holy writ proofs; but in the warm halls of the heart one single, untestified memory's spark shall suffice."[59] In this context *The Free States* may be read not only as an assent to those, like Fenimore Cooper, who increasingly conceded the impossibility of seclusion, but also as a repudiation of those who pretended that the union remained morally sound. That meant most politicians in America. As it shares with such a romance as *The Deerslayer* (1840) the perception that retreat no longer works, it sees also that the old hope for community has become a cheap appeal to the instinct for security. The cost of maintaining the myth of American unity is, according to Channing, the death of truth itself: to argue in unison that men can be property is as reasonable as for "a government to declare cotton to be horses, to write 'Horse' on all the bales . . and to set these down as horses in the custom house papers."[60] Delusion runs rampant in America; *The Free States* sees that the national disruption of the *Creole* case foretells a larger chaos, and Channing recoils from those who would forestall that chaos by pretending there is no cleavage in the land. "The alliance," Edward Everett insisted on July 4, 1830, "between labor and capital (which is nothing but labor saved) may truly be called a *holy alliance*."[61] The language of religion, like that of law, was degenerating in America into a cosmetic for the lines that cut society, lines too ugly to look at on independence day. In the same spirit, supporters of the Bank of the United States decried its opposers as victims of an irrational craze, a hysteria like anti-Masonism. In the clear light of reason, they said, the bank reveals itself as everyone's friend.[62]

In just this way, Secretary Webster's call for the return of the *Creole* slaves was an assertion that there was such a thing as American consensus, and that it was embodied in her laws. This Channing denies. Webster, to be sure, did not stand with the mythmakers; in fact his greatness rose with his candor; his legendary second reply to Senator Hayne (1830), in which he asserted that the idea of state immunity to federal law was treason, is a tough-minded appeal to the necessity for centralized discipline in a world of diverging interests. It sings of no love affair between labor and capital; it speaks the language of power and speaks it frankly. Webster's is a language that Channing knew well, for he himself had used it—risking the very foundation of his faith. Like Webster's, Channing's idea of truth had always partaken largely of the idea of utility; truth often seems in his pages a function of consequence. As Webster virtually rules out the possibility of ascertaining objective right and wrong on the question of the tariff, and insists on majority rule as the only insurance against catastrophe, so Channing railed against the trinity for its pernicious fragmentation of the feeble human capacity for worship.[63] In the same way he tried to prove the divine truth of Christianity by proving its earthly value. Christ, like the tariff, is true because he works.

The Duty of the Free States declares that this will no longer do. It says that the habit of measuring truth by utility—the habit Webster raised to new dignity and urgency—has driven men to conceal the meaning of their acts from themselves. Channing does not exempt himself from the charge, as the Follen and Dwight sermons show. And it is in *The Free States* that he declares both the illusion of national unity and the forced acquiescence to national policy to be morally unacceptable. It is a prophecy of civil war.

Channing had learned that American politics had a fearful symmetry. If he did not live to see the final battlelines, he had seen enough to know that Daniel Webster could swing from sectionalist to nationalist, and John Calhoun from nationalist to nullifier, in the space of a very few years. (To the man who wavered somewhere in between, Henry Clay, he had written with bitter reproach.) The burden was the fear that *any* man—the best of men—would adjust his principles to his needs. Even more frightening was the thought that in the process the distinction between principle and need could be lost for a whole culture. This is what Channing cried out against. When the "people's president" turned his administration inside out over the sexual reputation of Peggy O'Neale, when Whigs like Clay and Theodore Frelinghuysen sought to sour the people on Jackson by blasting the Sunday mails in accents of high-sounding piety, when the enemies of the United States Bank discovered the virtues of those banks which granted favorable interest rates to their own coterie, it could not be called an age of inspiring consistency. Too often, Channing found himself watching the spectacle of manipulation of the many by the few, on both sides of the Congressional aisle: " 'The generous zeal for freedom,' which has stirred and armed so many of our citizens to fight for Texas, turns out to be a passion for unrighteous spoil."[64] Channing could find no party to join. But he refused to stand aloof all the same.

What then could he do? He took the only course morally possible: he used his large prestige and spoke out publicly for civil disobedience. Only a vestige of equivocation remains as he all but urges defiance of the laws of restitution and condemns the Supreme Court ruling against trial by jury in cases of recovered runaway slaves. He demands immediate abolition of slavery in the District of Columbia, where Congress had jurisdiction. In spite of all his investment in order—his building-block theory of conversion, his fear of historical interruption, his halt before unchecked nature—Channing now calls for open challenge to "palpably unrighteous law." His grounds for this incitement are once again hermeneutic: the constitution, like the scripture, recedes into a role of confirming the insight of the righteous individual. There are no authorities any more except the internal sense of right, and this sense man has failed to transfer to his institutions. What Channing has lost under all the accumulated pressure of the slavery crisis is nothing less than his faith in objective standards, a loss that may be seen where deep change is always to be seen, in the language: "I do not . . . blame the slave for rising at any moment against his master. In so doing he would incur no guilt."[65] In the paragraph that contains these sentences, the word "guilt" is not used objectively, for Channing still stops short of urging slave rebellion; the word denotes rather what we would call guilty *feeling*. For the whole world of values has collapsed into the mind, and all Channing can do is fight to keep his own house in moral order, and to share, through public utterance, that fight with other men. Sometimes the drama of his struggle is manifest in the smallest moments, as here, where the almost invisible line between guilt as an objective quality and as an internal feeling signals that he has come to the very edge of exonerating the rebel. He cannot quite bring himself to say that to feel no guilt is to bear no guilt, because he understands the devastating antinomian consequences of that statement. Though he will not say it consciously, his language, formulated less than consciously, says it for him.

The conservative Unitarians saw that he had left them. The antislavery activists, including Mrs. Child, saw that he now stood with them, even if they could not conscript him into their party. If he had lived, he might have taken further steps toward

open political alliance with one or the other group—as he began
to do in leading the Faneuil Hall rally after the death of Elijah
Lovejoy, who had been murdered while defending his abolitionist press in Alton, Illinois. In the last weeks of 1838, John
Quincy Adams could write, "The Doctor was heretofore an idol
of the party now calling themselves Whigs, but has become very
obnoxious to them. They had almost worshipped him as a saint;
they now call him a Jacobin."[66] As it was, Channing died a man
whose deepest fears for America seemed destined to prove justified, a man who rejected both the temptation of individual retreat and the reassurance of collective action. He died as he had
lived—trying to find the right balance between them.

Channing had done what Alexander Pope could not do; he
had pursued the reincarnated Satan that the course of American
history offered him, and he had risked the dangers of pursuit.
Just before his death, through his last antislavery tracts, he expressed satisfaction with his choice—but it was satisfaction, not
complacence. Unlike many of those who moved with him, he
did not delude himself into thinking that evil could be expelled
by moral action. He knew Satan's limitless capacity to dis-
semble.

With this knowledge Channing finally met, and restated,
the central demand of Edwards, that a man must combat evil
while never ceasing to combat himself: "No enemy can do us
equal harm with what we do ourselves."[67] Channing understood, as had Pope and Edwards, that Satan's greatest power is
his capacity to convince men that he does not exist. That conviction, Channing saw, had already reigned in the America of 1840
for quite some time, and when it fell, it gave way to the equally
dangerous deception of believing that Satan exists in only one
place.

"As in our souls the conquest of one evil passion reveals to
us new spiritual foes, so in society one great evil hides in its
shadow others perhaps as fearful, and its fall only summons us

to new efforts."[68] Reading these patient words, and thinking of
the company that joins Channing in their warning, one wonders
if America in its very nature somehow nurtures a moral relativism. Our two great immigrant literatures, the Puritan of the
seventeenth century and the Jewish of the twentieth, both confirm the sense that moral clarity cannot be carried intact onto
America's shores. For Benjamin Franklin, always so representative, the conviction of sin becomes the confession of "errata." It
was a desire to escape this diminution, this reductionism, that
made the slaveholding South such a welcome enemy to the
troubled New Englanders of Channing's time.[69] As we have seen
by examining Channing's Newport and his Harvard, the
members of his generation were starved for causes. They were
victims, too, of their inherited rationalism. "Later Protestantism," Norman O. Brown has written, "loses Luther's historical
eschatology, his faith in the end of the world, and his hope that
it would come soon. And then the realistic recognition of the
dominion of the Devil and death in this world is no longer psychologically possible."[70] Molded by, if not an exemplar of, such
rational Protestantism, Channing knew that slavery offered a
way to restore that psychological possibility. The problem was
that it was too easy. He saw not only the truth in the Edwardsean legacy of spiritual combat but also (as Edwards himself discovered through the revivals that he launched) the danger of
abusing that activism. Channing said for his time what Reinhold
Niebuhr has said for ours—that the forgetting of evil is the catastrophe of modern man, but that if we remember it, we must remember that we *all* participate in it. The historical truth of that
insight for colonial America has been explored by Alan Heimert,
who demonstrates what a frightful demand it was in the century
in which Channing was born. Heimert's account of the evangelical movement as it pushed toward revolution is a chronicle of
repeated transformation (in the French and Indian War and later
in the Revolution) from sacrifice to vindictiveness and self-

praise. Heimert shows for the eighteenth century what Channing knew for the nineteenth, and what we must surely know for the twentieth: the tragic paradox that righteous struggle carries an inevitable aftermath of self-righteous pride.[71]

We have seen that many interlocking reasons made Channing a committed man but kept him from becoming a party man. He recognized the world of *The Rape of the Lock* and tried to reveal it to itself; he shared the activism of Edwards and his disciples but could not run with Bellamy's legions. If he had once observed the world with eyes like those of an Augustan, he left it with those of a grieved Victorian, consumed with the need to escape the self and the calculus of self-interest. "We must cease to count pleasures and pains," he wrote in 1840, "as if working a sum in arithmetic, or to weigh them against each other as in scales."[72] These words are a reminder that if Channing began in the company of Pope, he ended with J. S. Mill, fleeing like Mill from Jeremy Bentham's shadow. Consider Mill's joy as he emerges from his collapse, as he discovers the same pattern of rise and fall in human history as that which he has lived through himself: "The destiny of mankind in general was ever in my thoughts, and could not be separated from my own. I felt that the flaw in my life, must be a flaw in life itself."[73] This is not only the unique voice of a man coming to terms with his own freakish genius, but the general voice of a century sated with the self. It is Carlyle's, Arnold's, Newman's voice—and Channing should be added to their number. In the phrase of one student of transcendentalist individualism, Channing had come to find it "teleologically inadequate."[74] Looking toward the alternative escapes of individual self-reliance and what Arnold called "immolation" in history (the same word appears in *The Free States*), Channing's vertigo is the measure of his enduring human significance. He did not lay it bare for the world; he did not tell his own story except by indirection, by allowing his humanity to inform his politics, his criticism, his every word. And so others must tell it for him. If, on a journey through American letters, one reads through his works and grasps his presence, one will eventually arrive with a sense of familiarity at another statement of tragic dignity composed by an American Victorian. When one reads of Henry Adams batting against the walls of his ignorance and his inheritance, half in a wish to stop living, half in a wish to live more fully in the current of his times—one might then recall the divided Channing. When one reads of Adams, head in hands, sitting stunned on the steps of the Paris exposition hall in which the dynamo hummed "an audible warning to stand a hair's breadth further for respect of power—while it would not wake the baby lying close against its frame,"[75] one might think again of Channing—of his bound love and fear of nature's power. For like Adams, if not so beautifully as he, Channing asked the overwhelming question of his century and ours: whether the world is spinning into chaos, or, after long penance, tapping the divine. That question, which now as then elicits all the varying strategies of self-defense—embarrassment, indifference, and dogma— has rarely been asked with greater dignity.

5

Channing and Romanticism

Moderation is not the opposite of rebellion. Rebellion in itself is moderation, and it demands, defends, and re-creates it throughout history and its eternal disturbances. The very origin of this value guarantees us that it can only be partially destroyed. Moderation, born of rebellion, can only live by rebellion. It is a perpetual conflict, continually created and mastered by the intelligence. It does not triumph either in the impossible or in the abyss. It finds its equilibrium through them. Whatever we may do, excess will always keep its place in the heart of man, in the place where solitude is found. We all carry within us our places of exile, our crimes and our ravages. But our task is not to unleash them on the world; it is to fight them in ourselves and in others. Rebellion, the secular will not to surrender . . . is still today at the basis of the struggle. Origin of form, source of real life, it keeps us always erect in the savage, formless movement of history.

—Albert Camus

THE ACKNOWLEDGMENT of past masters in literature and art has always involved the emotional confusion of discipleship and grudging obligation, and since filial love is not a simple thing, there is challenge and value in describing it. Even with its opportunities for fantasy, the hunt for influence remains one of the ways in which we may try to hear the human dialogue. Common sense is important in such researches. The very unanimity, for example, with which Channing's generation of rational Christians acknowledged one master, John Locke, is and should remain a persuasion that they were right, that they recognized their lineage and avowed it. Still, the task of understanding Channing's divergence from his contemporaries can be completed only after a closer look at the Lockean heritage. In his restless obedience to Locke lie the clues to his discontent with the age into which he was born.

Locke's *Essay concerning Human Understanding* (1690) set the tone for a century, as one writer puts it, "with an almost scriptural authority."[1] It did so because it was an unprecedented gesture of explication, an agent of what Peter Gay has called the central objective of the Enlightenment: to "disenchant" the world.[2] The merciless assault on innate ideas that constitutes its first book is a declaration that the universe is comprehensible, and the place for mystery grows ever smaller as the *Essay* proceeds. No event of the mind, however abstract, lies beyond its power of dissection. Hours no less than minutes, years no less than days, large numbers and small, even the concept of infinity, may all be derived as aggregates of simple ideas. Too often described as prosaic, the *Essay* has a grandeur of discovery; it marvels at the mental universe that man can construct from the materials of sensation. With each passing chapter, the reader better understands how Locke could come to dominate an age, how first-rate thinkers could read him with transport, "gathering up handfuls of silver and gold, from [their] newly discovered treasure."[3]

In his humanism, Channing stood firmly in the Locke tradition, never abandoning the idea of the senses as man's window on creation. His lifelong loyalty to the miracles as a tether to God proves his constancy to the Lockean view. But as the romantic revolution attests, and as its historians insist, there was poison in Locke as well as sustenance. Love, hatred, joy, sorrow, hope, fear, despair, anger, envy are catalogued in two dense pages of the *Essay* as forms of self-interest; love is "the delight which any present or absent thing is apt to produce"; hatred is "the thought of pain".[4] Such a utilitarian frame of mind has never stirred the imagination and probably never will. The concomitant premise of a mechanistic world and the futility of searching the *Essay* for a truly prideworthy *homo faber* combine to balance, if not to cancel, its soaring power with a theme of human limits. But Locke's antagonism to the poetic spirit is easily and often exaggerated. Vital piety and a relish for beauty not only survived but sometimes incorporated the Lockean system, as the example of Jonathan Edwards shows. Channing, in the same way, never thoroughly condemned the image of man standing apart from nature. We have seen his tentative moves toward more romantic views of that relation, but even in these respects he remained a child of the eighteenth century.

There is, all the same, an unbridgeable distance between Locke's account of reality and Channing's. It is not so much the preference for an organic over a mechanistic world, though that is part of it; not so much a disappointment with the passive status of man, though that is part of it too. Channing's dissent— and this is absolutely crucial to understanding him—revolves rather around his fear that the Lockean world could not hold together, that built into it was the principle of its own disintegration. It is here that we find Channing's singularity, because his disappointment with Locke is not quite the same as Ripley's or Parker's or Emerson's, all of whom balked because they felt that the sensational doctrine defined a world *too* self-contained, too self-sufficient. Channing's difficulty is different, deeper, because he felt that the sensational doctrine posed a threat to human community. He was able to comprehend the inevitability of reaction against the cool doctrine of sensationalism, and thereby to anticipate the passionate efforts, even revolutions, that romanticism would sanction for supplying the missing principle of social cohesion.

Channing's first concern throughout his life was with the

imminence of social disunity, which he considered a potential
offshoot from the intellectual debates in which he participated.
His reluctance to insist without bounds on the validity of a personal reading of scripture, his wariness of westward expansion,
his prophecy of civil war, indeed his basic ambivalence toward
individual autonomy, are all expressions of the same alarm.
"Place a man alone . . . and his Power [lies] dormant and
inert."[5] The borders of Channing's America were rushing outward; even the titular capital shifted within his lifetime from
Philadelphia to New York to Washington; a growing empire is
one thing with a stable center; without one it is quite another.
Channing felt his world possessed by unchecked centrifugal
motion. What saved him from dogmatic conservatism, and what
keeps his voice alive for us, is his alertness to the possibility that
an enforced order might be imposed by those impatient with
confusion. He was very much aware that the appeal of authority
grows with the fact of division: "An espionage of bigotry," he
preached in 1830, "may as effectually close our lips and chill our
hearts, as an armed and hundred-eyed police."[6] Both possibilities were real to him. To do any kind of justice to Channing, we
must understand how he found and responded to both freedom
and constraint in the Lockean world that he felt to be his own.

One technique for discovering a man's basic assumptions
about the world is to notice what makes him laugh. Even the
Essay concerning Human Understanding harbors such clues of
humor, for it begins as a polemic and seeks to vanquish its opponents by implicating them in beliefs that it judges absurd: "To
suppose the soul to think, and the man not to perceive it is, as
has been said, to make two persons in one man."[7] The romantics
would render the idea of hidden mental function, of "two persons in one," considerably less comical, and the human mind
since Freud has been unrecognizable without such a notion of
doubleness. As we shall see, Locke by no means spoke without

psychological subtlety, but his view of man remained a unitary one. The *Essay* presents a creature for whom self-understanding is fully attainable through the exercise of reason. Though the idea of obscurity, the mind as a "dark closet," does appear in Locke, man's vision, according to the *Essay*, is attenuated with respect to things outside himself, not within. This conviction of the mind's penetrability and Locke's consequent refusal to think of man as internally divided are the first elements of the empirical tradition to which Channing could not fully assent. He could not because he was a Christian whose experience variously confirmed the subtle and constant workings of sin in human affairs. We have seen him confront again and again the reality of self-deception in himself and others, of duplicity and self-hatred. His sensitivity to such dualities is most evident in the battle over slavery, but his personal acquaintance with them dates back to the Newport, Richmond, and Harvard days. The remainder of his life did not unteach those early lessons.

Channing simply did not live in the world that Locke described, though the spokesmen for his culture said he did. Returning to Cambridge to take his divinity degree after the Richmond breakdown and Newport solitude, he soon found himself speaking a language of official euphemism. Preferring the smaller church on Federal Street to the prestigious one at Brattle Square, both of which sought his ministry, he said nothing of his uneasiness at the relaxed Brattle style of liberal doctrine, citing instead his delicate health as the basis for his decision. Channing was human, and being human he did not always say what he meant. This fact has import because this was a man extraordinarily sensitive to the infiltration of deceit into daily human discourse. A source of friction with himself, it made him feel and confess that he was indeed "two persons in one."

Settled in a large house on Berry Street, he wrote for his mother to join him. For her sake or his? Whose comfort was he securing? His biographers have debated such questions, but an answer to this kind of inquiry into motive is very hard to come by even from the most personal of his surviving utterances. "His discourses," wrote his nephew, "were his best diary."[8] To the extent that the discourses do record a process of self-analysis, their growing acknowledgment of human duplicity confirms the sense one derives from the simple outline of Channing's life, the sense that he became more and more convinced that men were at war within themselves.

"I am . . . little disposed," he wrote to his brother's widow in the summer of 1811, "to join with writers of fiction and exalt [children] to the ranks of angels."[9] This unsentimental judgment of childhood—another clue to Channing's Calvinist strain—is an overlooked element in the formation of his political opinions during the years of "Mr. Madison's war." Speaking of the young nation, he constructed an equation between youth and immaturity: "such is war; the youthful eye is dazzled with its ornaments; the youthful heart dances to its animated sound."[10] The young country, he declared, was entertaining itself with a violent show; and however naive or willfully ignorant he was of the political justification for exploiting such a zeal, his sermons were not the invective that some of his peers produced. Elijah Parish, for example, put it simply: "Your rulers . . . intend to lop off your limbs."[11] Channing's war sermons do find a place in his lifework—as efforts to broaden the definition of courage to include an idea of restraint as well as of boldness.

Channing's antiwar sermons did make their contribution to the Federalist howl over war with Mother Britain, but they are also, like so much of his polemical work, a combination of expedience with principle. In this sense they contributed to his ongoing self-examination. He felt uneasy in the role of Federalist partisan, and his growth into the maturity of doubt is clearly attested by the shift from the ecstatic celebration of Napoleon's exile to Elba (1814) to the deeply ambivalent essay on Napoleon written more than a decade later. These years show Channing's self-division, his growing sense that the truth is always evasive. All the while he took pains to distinguish pacifism from secession. In 1812 his rhetoric could encourage such confusion, but by 1814, in the darkest days of the war, he offered public prayer that God "will turn the invader from our shores."[12] The progressive softening of tone, the retractions of the later Napoleon essay, and above all the patriotic rationale of his dissent, all show the war years to have been a many-sided trial, another experience that weakened his faith in the rational and unitary nature of man.

Channing was variously discovering the "dark closet" of his soul, for which the Lockeans had no adequate explanation. In many respects his resolve against slavery became possible only because he conceded that such a tension did exist within him, because he was able to exorcise that part of him which had cried foul against Mr. Madison and fomented what some called treason. To a man whose instincts were for sober England over radical France, the War of 1812 was unconscionable. And Channing did deplore it. Elected a counsellor of the Massachusetts Peace Society in 1816, he preached a pacifism that continued to color his social writings for twenty years, and in his refrains on "gradual reform" the adjective was as important as the noun. And so it is all the more noteworthy that his late years saw him turn against those who applauded loudest at his restraint. In this sense his emergence as an ally of the abolitionists was the fullest kind of personal achievement, a rising above the instincts of the self. Even in his headstrong days as a Federalist spokesman, he could not always sustain the necessary distance between his two selves: once, in the sitting room of a bereaved parishioner whose child had died in agonizing fever, he began to utter the expected words of solace only to burst into tears. Those who wanted a mouthpiece of condolence grew discontented with him; those who loved his inability to sustain dishonesty loved him more.

Channing did not surrender to self-love over time. He took

more and more account of the strength of his secret will, which had its sway even against exposure by the conscious judgment: "Let me avoid every feeling of rivalship," he wrote to Samuel Thacher ten years into his ministry. But when his greatest rival, Buckminster, died at the height of his powers, Channing's letters express an excessive solicitousness for the abandoned flock. The surviving institution, he laments, will not draw them to God as had the departed man.[13] But this is not the core of his response; he was buffeted by the conflicting feelings of any man whose burden is lightened by another man's death. Accepting the Dexter lectureship, which Buckminster had held, he purchased Buckminster's books at auction, began to employ them, then resigned before speaking a word from Buckminster's podium. It is a tale of tentative, self-dividing actions.

The internal debate over slavery marks the culmination of a life of growing self-recognition. And the more Channing came to know himself, the more enemies he made. He found both the theorists and the practitioners of his world indifferent to the contention he felt in his soul. Bit by bit he disengaged himself from his congregation, first by lobbying for an assistant, then by engineering reductions in his own salary. The climax came in 1840 when the Federal Street church committee refused permission for the Massachusetts Anti-Slavery Society to hold a memorial for Charles Follen under its roof. Channing speeded now toward dissolution of their bond (the letters strikingly recall those of his uncle Henry in New London). He could not hide his bitterness: "Is there not a secret understanding, that the ministry, while it condemns sin in the mass, must touch gently the prejudices, wrongs, and abuses which the community has taken under its wing?"[14] In thirty-seven years of pastorship, he had failed to break the shell of complacence. His words to the proprietors are barely tinged with reproach; fiercely polite, they record a sad man's valediction. "Our family is falling to pieces," he had written when death took his sister; "is there no bond of union?"[15]

Now he carried this question into the sphere of his lifetime labor, for the community he served seemed built on sand. John Locke had proven much too right: words, as Locke had said, bore no necessary connection to the ideas they described. Custom did rule the world. The words of proper Boston became for Channing merely clusters of obnoxious sound.

Up and down New England now they called him Reverend, a title he disliked. In Lenox, where he lodged after his exhausting work on *The Duty of the Free States*, his hosts addressed him with incessant reverence while they walked in the Berkshire hills. His private writings on nature always dwell longer than his public words on the pleasures of the eye:

> We discovered a noble range of mountains, their declivities toward us thrown into shade, and their waving outline, gentle and beautiful, forming an affecting contrast with their grandeur and solemnity . . . Below them was a sheet of water of considerable extent . . . the more distant part of it darkened by eminences beyond, and the part nearest to us brightened by the sun's light, which fell on it through a soft mist. The mist was dense enough to be impressed with the shadows of trees on the neighbouring heights, so as to give a singular mixture of light and shade in its thin and ethereal substance, yet not so dense as to prevent a dim, visionary reflection of the trees in the tranquil surface of the water.[16]

Amid a mixture of transfixing beauty and pious chatter he learned that the anniversary of British abolition had been forgotten. When reminded, no one cared. His last public words were published as *Emancipation*: "Had I been solicited," he said, "I probably should not have consented to speak. Had I found here a general desire to celebrate this day . . . I should have held my peace. But finding that no other voice would be raised . . . I trust you will accept with candor what I have been obliged to prepare in haste, and what may have little merit but that of pure intention."[17] He managed only a few more miles after the Lenox effort. The inn where he died still stands in Bennington, Vermont, and a stone memorial overlooks the gentle landscape that seems, from a distance at least, unspoiled.

The balanced, lucid world of Locke, inhabited by men in harmony with their environment and with themselves, became less and less recognizable to Channing through the years. As a consequence, he drifted from those of his peers who clung to such a world. Though he sometimes wished to reverse this motion, it could not be reversed by the application of his intellect because it was instigated by his experience, by a life of examination into the ambiguity of motive. The flight from Locke, which was never a narrow quarrel, but an antipathy to a way of thinking, began as much in Channing's head as in his heart. The *Essay Concerning Human Understanding*, in many ways the Unitarian Bible,[18] provoked in him the opposite of confidence.

In the same empirical tradition with Bacon, who had called truth "the daughter of time," Locke narrated a tale whose hero is time, for the possibility of human contact depends on the slow accretion of symbols by which men can communicate to each other their disparate experience. Locke is very stern in denying that the emergence of speech in a human child signifies any kind of a priori knowledge. On the contrary, the advent of language marks the beginning of an individual's effort to save himself from the isolation in which he is born. Reading the *Essay*, one feels the urgency with which men seek to escape themselves, to gather under a protective canopy of common knowledge—an assembly made possible only by the miracle of language. The empirical philosophy, or the "mechanical," as its romantic opponents would sneeringly call it, thus provided for human fellowship. But it did so always with a shiver, precipitated by the conviction that so much—all civilization, all progress—rested on such delicate mechanisms as perception and speech. Indeed Locke's notion of a normal human being is one who walks a tightrope between madness and idiocy. This is where his psychological insight is truly remarkable. If the power of abstraction becomes too strong, if it yokes alien experiences violently together and gives them a common name, then the territory of madness has been entered.[19] (Literary critics increasingly acknowledged that genius was not far away.) If, on the other hand, the power of abstraction becomes too feeble, such that each pellet of sensation must be lengthily pondered without a grasp of its likeness to others, then the mind has fallen into the pathetic dullness of stupidity. Such a perilous balance was Locke's legacy, and the battles of Channing's life—most conspicuously the struggle over scripture—manifest the crisis that Locke engendered. As we have seen, the real issue behind the exegetical debates was the means for holding men in contact with each other. Channing's orthodox opponents insisted that the Bible, because of its essential changelessness, was a kind of polar star by which men could get their bearings in a spinning world. Though Channing was willing to contemplate something less than fixity in scripture, he could never bring himself to relinquish the lifeline of the miracles. He could never release man from all external signposts, because he did not trust the guidance of the liberated soul. It was Channing's experience of life, his personal knowledge of the human heart, that stopped him from embracing the romantic alternative to Locke. In considering that fact, it is well to bear in mind that Emerson, who is often credited with a wisdom of which Channing is supposed innocent, was never truly a pastor.

We have seen that Francis Hutcheson answered a fundamental need for Channing in his youth, a need to believe in some kind of internal sense by which men can find their just relation to each other. Locke, or at least those who drilled Locke into Channing and his Harvard classmates, offered a marionette-man; too much human activity was called reflex, too little inhered in man by which he could know and understand his brethren. This misconception Channing sought to rectify. His great capacity for sympathy led him to strain, sometimes to the edge of bathos, for a sense of contact, a connectedness to life that Locke did not provide. Irving Babbitt, who was more than normally mindful that this sort of sympathy can ignore the distinction between the human and the subhuman, used an unkind phrase to evaluate this awakened power of identification. "The rehabilitation of the ass," he called the stirrings of benevolence in the "age of feeling," comparing it with "the malady of those who neglect the members of their own family and gush over animals."[20] The harshness of Babbitt's judgment does not vitiate its value; Channing did indeed participate in a push for sympathy that could at times become hysterical. But it is important to see that the Lockeans had starved him for such feeling; he was disposed therefore to welcome the counterdoctrine that man possessed an identity before and beyond experience. "[Richard] Price," he declared, referring to a Welsh philosopher who had refined Hutcheson's doctrine of the indwelling moral sense, "saved me from Locke's Philosophy."[21] What distinguishes Channing from others who welcomed such a doctrine is once again that he believed this identity capable of descent as well as ascent, that he recognized an internal Satan as well as an internal God, and that he understood the close relation of the two.

Channing paced in the prison described by the interpreters of Locke. He could not contemplate without protest the exclusion of man from the heart of nature's workings, nor could he accept the equal punishment of exile from other human beings. He was revived and invigorated by the romantic rebellion; we must therefore consider why he refused it.

The generalization may be risked that the romantic mind was repelled above all by the specter of mechanism in eighteenth-century thought. It was further inflamed by the threat to human connectedness. One of the essential points of romanticism is its rejection of the idea that human beings depend for their linkage on a chain of experience; it seeks instead an inward principle independent of experience, which can unite men beyond severance. Outside England, the work of Leibniz and his popularizer Christian Wolff had long challenged Locke on the grounds that the sensational doctrine could not account for human creativity: "To vindicate the existence within us of the principles of necessary truth," wrote Leibniz in the year of Locke's death, "is also to distinguish man from the brutes."[22] Thus the German tradition of organicism, culminating in Kant, was able to deny Locke a European hegemony. But the prestige of empiricism in England, incalculably enlarged by Newton, tended to force dissent into eccentric and self-conscious forms. Already in the century of Newton and Locke, Blake set new standards of irreverence toward the mechanistic view of the world and the mind, and loneliness became the poets' theme. Yet in England one finds the clearest expression of anxiety at the problem of isolation not in verse but in fictional prose. The narrators of Defoe are perhaps the most obvious examples—cut off by plague, by shipwreck, or in the case of Moll Flanders by converting the body into barter. The fragility of human exchange, the power of the word—misunderstood, or overheard, or interrupted—deeply to alter human lives would continue to furnish the novelists' theme at least through Jane Austen. But perhaps the most penetrating study of isolation in English prose is a less canonical product of the preromantic years—Sterne's *The Life and Adventures of Tristram Shandy* (1760-61).

Sterne, whom Channing read in college, populates the world with dazed amnesiacs, most memorably, Uncle Toby in his backyard trenches trying to grasp a receding past. There is inexhaustible wit in Sterne's parody: Mrs. Shandy, whose husband precedes their monthly coitus by winding the living-room clock, "could never hear the said clock wound up,—but the thought of some other things unavoidably popp'd into her head,—& *vice versa:*—Which strange combination of ideas the sagacious *Locke*, who certainly understood the nature of these things better than most men, affirms to have produced more wry actions than all other sources of prejudice whatsoever." The laughter here is precious, for it is all that makes bearable the appalling loneliness of the Lockean vision as Sterne interprets it: "[Mrs. Shandy] went out of the world at last without knowing whether [the earth] turned *round*, or stood *still*." However hoarse her husband grows in his prattling, he can never convey the spin of the planet to her as a fact with the feel of experience; it remains a phrase without an idea: "My father had officiously told her above a thousand times which way it was,—but she always forgot."[23] His rage, her shame, and the consequent silence between them, are another joke—clever, allusive, but ultimately beyond laughter. This is the collapse that the romantics refused to accept as inevitable. It is also, in essence if not in intensity, a version of Channing's personal experience. He too felt more and more as if he were talking to himself in a hopelessly private language.

The problem of isolation as dramatized by Sterne required for its solution a radically revised version of the human mind, and this responsibility the chief romantic spokesmen readily acknowledged. Pronouncing the epic scale of their restorative programs, Emerson in *Nature* (1836) declared that "the reason why the world lacks unity, and lies broken and in heaps, is because man is disunited with himself." Wordsworth began *The Prelude* (1805) with a grand epic voice, and Kant *The Critique of Pure Reason* (1781) with the promise of a new "Copernican revolution." The war against Locke was declared.

Despite this unanimity of ambition, there is, as Arthur Lovejoy implied in his famous essay "On the Discrimination of Romanticisms," a plurality inherent in the romantic idea itself. This must be so because of the nature of the movement as a declaration of independence from externals. Since uniformity and the holiness of duplication by one mind of another are exactly the premises that the new philosophy condemned, license for diversity resides in the core of the rebellion. Unfair as the school of Babbitt has been in attacking that declaration of independence, there are real grounds for questioning the feasibility of its social application. Channing saw those grounds, saw that the impulse to reject sensationalism might give rise to a new and different kind of solitude.

The divergence between romantic ambition and accomplishment is often striking, not least in the cherished project of promoting human community. Though Channing never had the opportunity to read the poem in which Wordsworth most fully describes "love of nature leading to love of man," he certainly grasped that his age was proffering that hope above all other hopes. "A great moral revolution," he writes in the 1839 letter to Jonathan Phillips, "is making its way through society," and its egalitarian objectives are "the master-movement of the age."[24] But Channing ended his life doubtful that the romantic version of mind could insure its fulfillment any more than Locke had done.

It is not hard to see the reason for his uncertainty, since to resolve that doubt remains the critical challenge for every reader of the manifesto of English romanticism, Wordsworth's *Prelude*. The very need of that poem to articulate with Miltonic solemnity the natural origins of human fellowship underscores the condition of estrangement in which it was composed. Wordsworth felt, as one critic puts it, "a suffocating, almost panicky fear that man is doomed to isolation."[25] His candor gives us a perpetual stranger; in country and in city he stands apart. It may be a milkmaid's song to which he cannot open himself, or in France he may earn "the indulgence that a half-learnt speech / Wins from the courteous" (IX, 192-193), or in London he may face a wall of silence:

> .... a blind Beggar ......
> ....
> Wearing a written paper, to explain
> His story, whence he came, and who he was.
> ....
> This label seemed of the utmost we can know,
> Both of ourselves and of the universe.
>
> (VII, 639-646)

The Prelude is an anthology of truncated speech, of half-con-summated emotion. Before its travelers have realized that the Alps lie behind rather than before them, the mountains have been crossed. This is the emotional pattern of the whole: hope yielding disappointment. Still, these are no more than instances of the salutary tension that makes the poem great, vestiges of the torpor under attack. The pressing critical question in reading *The Prelude*, and in contemplating the whole romantic program for man, is whether a resort to private recollection of the kind Wordsworth recommends can cope with the underlying problem: what we now call alienation. The prevailing judgment has been that *The Prelude* does rise into spiritual triumph, but Wordsworth's poetry has also generated passionate attacks. This "minority" tradition, as one of its most distinguished exponents has called it, has challenged us to consider whether the reestablishment of human contact at the close of *The Prelude* may not fall short of authentic love, whether the poet does not retire into a world barely less private than that in which he begins. "The 'Intimations of Immortality,' " writes Douglas Bush, with his usual pointed good sense, "records a very individual kind of depression and a very individual solution."[26] Similarly, the "spots of time" that revive the poet of *The Prelude* are, by their very nature, exclusive. In the age of Beckett we are not unwilling to cite the act of writing itself as a sufficient denial of nihilism, and Wordsworth's public confessions are modern in exactly this sense, as efforts to avoid the fate of silence.

The Prelude has always provoked an astonishing range of response. It seems the destiny of romantic art to bring down upon itself every sort of critical passion, from worship to disgust, and this destiny is inextricably tied up with the romantic account of mind. The liberating discovery that *The Prelude* commemorates and seeks to duplicate—that the mind brings itself to bear on what it sees—is in itself a subverter of fixed meaning, in art as in life. Forming and formed by its object, the romantic version of mind destroys the model of man as receptacle. An incontrovertible consequence of such a view is a strident individualism, for readers as well as emperors. Channing spent his life watching this shift from object to subject: in theology, from God to man; in aesthetics, from the work of art to its effect; in education, from the body of knowledge to the student. The potential for individual isolation in such a newly structured world cannot be exaggerated, for the romantic shift brought to every man the fearsome responsibility of freedom. Moreover, the relativism in the romantic view has grown with time. In our century relativism has become virtually an epistemological assumption and threatens to become an ethical assumption as well. To be sure, the romantic prophets themselves possessed a kind of immunity to relativism, but one that has not proven heritable: "Kant," as R. G. Collingwood has written, "unquestioningly assumes [the mind whose workings he describes in the Critiques] to be the only kind of human mind that exists or ever has existed."[27] There is comfort in that faith; indeed one needs something like it to believe at all in the possibility of communication. (We should remember that Kant did turn very soon after the *Critique of Pure Reason* to the task of establishing a moral absolute in a world he had helped to make fluid.) But in our historicist age we no longer believe what Kant believed, though there are signs of resurgence of such a view, the view that C. S. Lewis calls "the doctrine of the unchanging human heart."[28] However safe they were from their own impli-

cations, the romantics did carry the seed of relativism, and
Channing knew it: "I apprehend that there is no such thing as
naked truth, at least not as far as moral subjects are concerned."[29] That knowledge was a burden all his life.

The close relation between romanticism and political revolution is an intimacy we feel even if we cannot quite define why
it should exist. "There is," writes Herbert Marcuse in *Reason and
Revolution*, "a necessary transition from Kant's analysis of the
transcendental consciousness to his demand for the community
of *Weltbürgerreich*, from Fichte's concept of the pure ego to his
construction of a totally unified and regulated society; and from
Hegel's idea of reason to his designation of the state as the union
of the common and the individual interest."[30] Students of America's origins may ratify Marcuse's insight by considering such
Puritan ideologues as John Preston, John Cotton, and Edwards—all possessed by visions of holy community, and all dis-
tinguishable from their contemporaries by their striking antipathy to mechanical models for the mind, their insistence on describing the mind with organic metaphor. Trees and fountains,
not clocks and engines, fill their psychological vocabulary: precisely the distinction by which recent scholarship, most notably
by M. H. Abrams in *The Mirror and the Lamp* and *Natural
Supernaturalism*, has divided classic from romantic. Indeed it
sometimes seems that an organic view of mind may serve as a
preliminary sign—not foolproof, but helpful—for finding the
political ideal of a given thinker. With due care, then, we may
permit ourselves to speak of such a thing as a romantic temperament outside the limiting dates usually assigned to the movement. And while its ultimate legacy may be one of fragmentation, even chaos, the romantic idea in its purest form carries a
passion for human fellowship.

Channing remained sensitive all his life to that paradox. He
must be distinguished from his peers by the fact that he was hard
pressed, even agonized, in choosing between the promise of a

new human community and the familiar world of temperate, wary individuals. It is the most vulnerable kind of historiography to speak of a man's predictive power, but it seems worth the risk to say that Channing would not have been surprised to witness Emerson's youthful zeal turning into the anguish of a lonely sage. "Two human beings," Emerson writes in his middle age, "are like globes, which can touch only in a point." What makes *Experience* such an affecting essay is its grieved acknowledgement of a lost capacity for human contact. This is the dark side of that Emersonian mood which also yields more strident phrases: "Nothing is at last sacred but the integrity of your own mind."[31] Emerson moves between such exultation and fatigue, but in both moods he remains a committed individualist.

Channing was not—as his last years show—an armchair judge. He did not pronounce the contest between classic and romantic a draw, nor did he congratulate himself on a proud neutrality. He shared and saved the essence of the romantic dream while enlisting himself not in a program of self-therapy but in political action. So often those who began in romantic optimism ended in a paralyzed reaction; the soured hopes of *The Prelude* are again exemplary. How Channing avoided that fate, how he kept disillusion from killing his sense of social obligation, is the balance of his story.

"Sin, in its true sense, is the violation of duty."[32] Channing's ethics are not complicated. But their purity is an achievement, not an evasion. We might borrow a phrase recently made current, and call this idea of virtue a "voluntary, inspired self-restraint."[33] Its component of self-denial is the moral analogue of Channing's wariness before an aesthetic that deifies nature, and this imperative, which is the key to understanding his politics, may be most clearly seen by returning one last time to the essays on Milton and Napoleon.

The study of Milton is a composite of romantic themes: "though sightless, he lived in light; . . . the soul, possessed and moved by . . . mighty though infant energies, is perpetually stretching beyond what is present or visible, struggling against the bounds of its earthly prison-house, and seeking relief and joy in imaginings of unseen and ideal being." The function of poetry becomes more than to "lift the mind above ordinary life." Poetry is a natural expression of the human spirit, an effect of which the soul is the cause. Exulting at the rapidity and capaciousness of Milton's mind, Channing anticipates the equivalence Emerson would draw between poet and hero, and speaks of what Emerson would later call that "gleam of light which flashes across [the] mind from within."[34]

If we keep in mind this manifold thrill of power, it becomes possible to see how closely the Napoleon essay follows in theme as well as in time: "Bonaparte obeyed the laws of progress, to which the highest minds are peculiarly subjected; and acquisition inflamed, instead of appeasing, the spirit of dominion." Poet and Emperor are similarly gifted, a parallel that Channing makes quite explicit: "[Napoleon's] intellect was distinguished by rapidity of thought. He understood by a glance what most men, and superior men, could learn only by study. He darted to a conclusion rather by intuition than reasoning." What, then, makes the all-important difference between hero and despot? It is not enough to say that Channing admired power only in the service of contemplation, for we know that he moved toward the life of action in his last years, that he condemned political indifference and was angered by the genteel. There is a sense in which he describes Napoleon's sweep through Europe as a poetry transformed into act—but the moral distinction between Milton and Bonaparte is not the simple difference between imagination and action. It is a difference in kind, not in form. Once again Channing's education in the idea of depravity is the key. Just as it prevented him from conceding that sensationalism could adequately explain human behavior, it restrains him now from assent: "[Though] the turpitude of an evil agent is diminished by infelicities of education or condition, we must not therefore confound the immutable distinctions of right and wrong, and withhold our reprobation from atrocities . . . the rapid and inventive intellect of Bonaparte was depraved."[35] There in all its starkness is a refusal of debate, an appeal beyond expression. The perseverance of the Puritan ethos is nowhere more striking than in such a resort to the ineffable quality of the damned. We have seen Channing's extreme reluctance to assume the responsibility of arbiter, his struggle against the temptation to locate sin outside the self. The same elements that have earned him the charge of timidity are those which vindicate his willingness to indict.

"[Bonaparte] claimed inspiration, and a commission from God . . . the massacre of Jaffa is universally known."[36] Channing believed that the moral distinction between Milton and Napoleon involved the difference between consent and resistance to this linkage of cause and consequence. He recognized that inspiration was ascribed more and more in his time to the agency of nature and furthermore that there was massacre everywhere in nature. Virtue required not an averting of the eyes but a rejection of the vision. This is the meaning of self-restraint in Channing: the capacity of man to hold himself beyond the reach of nature. And thus we may see his deep affinity with the chief romantic spirits of his age—even with Whitman, whose greatest poem devolves into an ode to duty after an orgy of sensation:

> On all sides prurient provokers stiffening my limbs,
> . . . .
> Depriving me of my best as for a purpose
> . . . .
> Deluding my confusion with the calm of the sunlight and pasture-fields,

. . . .
The sentries desert every other part of me

"You villain touch," completes the cry against a sensory bombardment in which beauty has become pain. No less than Whitman, Channing has earned that right of protest.

Wordsworth wrote his *Ode to Duty* (1804) concurrently
with *The Prelude*; Kant's came in stages after the *Pure Reason*,
culminating in the *Critique of Practical Reason* (1788); between
Werther (1774) and *Wilhelm Meister* (1796) there are twenty
years. But all such pairs, however long in the making, are indivisible wholes. The romantic liberation of mind from externals
inevitably fosters a need for some form of moral restraint,
though not always in the liberators themselves. And to defer an
answer to that need—as Channing well knew—is to create the
condition in which legislators unfriendly to human liberty
thrive. The insistence that duty must be divorced from natural
inclination finds its aesthetic corollary in Kant's theory of the
sublime—a quality attendant, for Kant as for Channing, upon
man's capacity to feel the immunity of the rational to the
natural. Kant's description of man as a creature determined in
the realm of nature but free in the world of morality found eager
audience in America. This is James Marsh, who brought the
Aids to Reflection to American readers: "Brutes are possessed of
various natures, some innocent or useful, otherwise noxious, but
all alike irresponsible in a moral point of view. But why? Simply
because they act in accordance with their natures." Such a conflict between nature and freedom recalled New Englanders to the
memory of their own past, stirring what remained of their
"Augustinian strain of piety." It is significant that Marsh directs
his readers backward beyond Bacon to the age of Augustine, to a
frankly medieval separation of matter from spirit, in which, he
promises, the lost union between philosophy and religion may
be found.[37] In America, as Perry Miller insisted, the "transcen-

dental" movement was at bottom religious, and risen from domestic roots.

Even in Channing we occasionally hear a call to mortify the flesh: "I may lose limb after limb, and in a certain time shall change every particle of my present frame, but I, myself, shall be unmutilated, and uncompounded, and undivided whole . . . My body is mine, not myself."[38] But such a dualism was finally anathema to him; he was too much a child of Locke to say, with Kant's great predecessor Leibniz, that "monads have no windows." And yet he was too much a Christian to admit unqualified identification of man with nature. He could not deny the intercourse between spirit and body, though he tried, especially during his spartan year in Richmond. And though he could not deny it, he sought heroically to control it. This was his idea of virtue, a faith in man's capacity to blend his spiritual and material selves. It has its aesthetic expression in his celebration of prose as a form capable of containing without confining emotion. What Santayana said of "transcendental" criticism, however far it may diverge from a true estimate of Emerson, is exactly what Channing refused to permit: "[Emerson] read transcendentally, not historically, to learn what he himself felt, not what others might have felt before him."[39] Channing's value to us as a critic is above all his insistence on keeping open the lines of human communication over time. He refused to admit that the self and the present are the only safe dimensions. Thus to him an act of true literary criticism is the confrontation by one mind of another, the contemplation of spirit *within* form. Friedrich Schiller, who died as Channing began his adulthood, put it this way: "Through Beauty the sensuous man is led to form and to thought; through Beauty the spiritual man is brought back to matter and restored to the world of sense."[40] Channing did not, as Schiller did, articulate this ideal for the ages, but he shared it, and his efforts to defend it are worthy of respect.

"The mind," Channing wrote in his study of Milton, "may

seem lawless in [the workings of poetry]; but it observes higher laws than it transgresses; . . . a great mind is the master of its own enthusiasm."[41] It is this capability of control that finally distinguishes Milton from Napoleon; its supreme triumph comes with Milton's depiction of Satan, whose virtues—courage, energy, eloquence—are harnessed by the poet, not released. Channing would have insisted that Blake was wrong on Milton's secret loyalty, that Milton created a siren but did not yield to her.

Channing's notion of virtue as power must, finally, be carefully distinguished from the idea of withdrawal, which he fought in himself over the course of his life. He advocated not sanctuary within the self but, as he calls it in *The Duty of the Free States*, "individual responsibility . . . which is very much lost."[42] He understood that romantic individualism would find a special receptiveness in America, that it could thrive in a culture that had shamed into silence most candid partisans of class allegiance. Like Tocqueville, Channing saw—and he most clearly expressed his insight in *The Free States*—that the American prohibition against class ideology would sanction a force of potentially greater disruption: what Quentin Anderson has called the "imperial self." The egalitarian idea can authorize personal ambition in a way that the hierarchical can never do; ascent is proscribed for no one. It is this situation that makes Benjamin Franklin's *Autobiography* such a curious psychological paradox and a quintessential American document: Franklin openly dislikes the rising men around him, all of whom resemble Franklin himself. Franklin's text confirms that the new nation harbored enormous reserves of competitive animus between men who had no quarrel with each other's principle, only with each other's success. This is what Channing saw. He saw Americans defining themselves not by beliefs but by interests, even such men as Hopkins, Whittier, Webster. In incipient form, this is the fundamental radical critique of democracy. For Channing

it was a sad discovery that "[Christ] is to be approached by gradual self-crucifixion."[43] He tried in his way to elevate the discourse of politics, to add his voice to that "Jacksonian impulse
[which] was . . . recalling Americans to the knowledge that
there were and ought to be essential differences among them."[44]
Because the periodic rise of frank individualism in America so
often seems a solace from national failure, Channing did not
want to believe in the universal dominion of self-interest. That
hypocrisy binds the American body politic is a conclusion he arrived at with reluctance, while for us it has achieved the status of
an expected premise. It has become part of our self-image, and
its presence tends to obscure the pain with which nineteenth-century Americans came upon it. We are told today from every
quarter that America's true religion is a religion of the self; to
Channing—and from Channing—this was news; for he, he himself confessed, had been an unwitting priest of that religion.

"If the walls of home are the bulwarks of a narrow, clannish
love, through which the cry of human miseries and wrongs
cannot penetrate, then it is mockery to talk of their sacredness."
What makes Channing's life finally so moving is his confession
that he too had forgotten and would again forget the fact of
complicity. In his ministry, indeed in his religion—for which he
apologized with a utilitarian defense—he was conscious that he
shared the sin for which he condemned Napoleon: living "for
effect." But the testimony of those who heard him, and the experience of reading him now, persuade that his effect was an
elevating one. Believing in "the intimate connexion of better and
juster views of human nature with all social and religious progress," he insisted that by conceiving of man as above brutality
one might help to make him so. He spoke with hope but without
fantasy about the human future: "The next general war will be a
war not of nations but of principles; absolutism must measure
swords with liberalism, despotism with free constitutions; and
from this terrible encounter both parties recoil. We indeed be-

lieve, that, with or without war, liberal principles and institutions are destined to advance, to make the conquest of Europe; and it is thought that these, being recognitions of human rights, will be less prodigal of human blood than absolute power."[45] We owe it to Channing to recognize the fervency of this moderated hope. He asked his contemporaries, and his posterity, only to choose civilization over barbarism. He hoped that man, despite his pride and his infinite capacity for self-deception, would find the restraint by which he could refuse to make himself a surrogate for God. Channing feared that such presumption could yield something hideous, and so he urged that men, through the difficult achievement of self-knowledge, should live content with their humanity. His example makes that objective less a surrender, and more an ambition.

Notes

PROLOGUE: FAMILY, CHILDHOOD, YOUTH

1. Edwards A. Park, "Memoir of Samuel Hopkins," in *The Works of Samuel Hopkins*, ed. Park (Boston, 1854), I, 83.

2. George Gibbs Channing, *Early Recollections of Newport* (Boston, 1868), p. 23.

3. Ibid., pp. 71-72.

4. W.I. Ward "George Whitefield," in *Early Religious Leaders of Newport* (Newport: Newport Historical Society, 1918), p. 119.

5. George Gibbs Channing, *Recollections*, pp. 164, 174, v, 42.

6. Edward Tyrrel Channing, *The Life of William Ellery*, in Jared Sparks, ed., *Library of American Biography* (Boston, 1836), VI, 87.

7. Emerson, *Nature* (1836). George Eliot, *Middlemarch* (1872).

8. George Gibbs Channing, *Recollections*, p. 267.

9. Letter from William Ellery to Channing, 10 July 1794 (Massachusetts Historical Society — abbreviated hereafter as MHS).

10. MHS Collections, 7th ser. (1914), vol. 9, I, no. 69, p. 373. Franklin B. Dexter, ed., *The Literary Diary of Ezra Stiles* (New York: Scribners, 1901), II, 459.

11. MHS Collections, 7th ser. (1914), vol. 9, I, no. 69, pp. 365, 369, 422. Morris Gutstein, *The Story of the Jews of Newport* (New York: Bloch, 1936), pp. 192-193.

12. G. Mason, ed. *Annals of Trinity Church*, 2nd ser. (Newport 1894), p. 318; 1st ser. (Newport, 1890), p. 223.

13. William Henry Channing, *Memoir of William Ellery Channing* (Boston, 1848), I, 13, 16. Cited hereafter as WHC, *Memoir*.

14. Ibid., I, 15.

15. Ibid., I, 16.

16. Letter from William Ellery to Channing, 22 April 1795 (MHS).

17. George Gibbs Channing, *Recollections*, p. 77.

18. Edward Tyrrel Channing, *Life of Ellery*, pp. 148-149.

19. See WHC, *Memoir*, I, 7-8. George Gibbs Channing, *Recollections*, p. 215.

20. Edward Tyrrel Channing, *Life of Ellery*, pp. 148-149, 94, 156, 150.

21. *Pennsylvania Magazine of History and Biography*, 11, no. 3 (Oct. 1887), pp. 318, 322.

22. W. R. Staples, *Rhode Island in the Continental Congress* (Providence, 1870), pp. 237-238, 95, 121, 106, 521, 105.

23. See H. James Henderson, *Party Politics in the Continental Congress* (New York: McGraw-Hill, 1974), p. 327; Lynn Montross, *Reluctant Rebels* (New York: Harper, 1950), pp. 318-319, 334; and Irwin Polishook, *Rhode Island and the Union* (Evanston: Northwestern University Press, 1969), p. 99.

24. Staples, *Rhode Island*, pp. 266, 532, 536-537.

25. The dispute was ostensibly over the duration of their terms.

26. Staples, *Rhode Island*, p. 98.

27. George Gibbs Channing, *Recollections*, p. 28.

28. WHC, *Memoir*, I, 20.

29. Ibid.

30. Ann Douglas, *The Feminization of American Culture* (New York, Knopf, 1977).

31. William Ellery Channing, *Works*, 6 vols, (Boston, 1848), IV, 337.

32. WHC, *Memoir*, I, 23.

33. Ibid., I, 22.

34. Channing, *Works*, IV, 336.

35. WHC, *Memoir*, I, 42, 37, 25, 24. Letter from William Ellery to Channing, 29 January 1795 (MHS).

36. Quoted in George Fredrickson, *The Inner Civil War* (New York: Harper, 1968), p. 33.

37. WHC, *Memoir*, I, 39.

38. G. S. Hillard, ed., *Memoir and Correspondence of Jeremiah Mason* (Cambridge, 1873), p. 8.

39. F. B. Dexter, ed., *Literary Diary of Ezra Stiles* (New York: Scribner's, 1901), III, 505.

40. E. E. and E. M. Salisbury, *Family Histories and Genealogies* (New Haven, 1892), I, 80, 79.

41. Stiles, *Literary Diary*, III, 274-275.

42. Henry Channing, *God Admonishing his People of their Duty, as Parents and Masters* (New London, 1786), pp. 25, 19.

43. "Mr. Channing practiced the halfway covenant in its extreme form; that is he admitted persons to membership in the church who

claimed no experience of the new birth." S. L. Blake. *The Later History of the First Church of Christ, New London* (New London: Press of the Day, 1900), p. 255. Inferences of revival have been based on the increase in communicants.

44. Salisbury, *Genealogies*, p. 80.

45. Henry Channing, *God Admonishing his People*, p. 21.

46. Salisbury, *Genealogies*, pp. 81, 82.

47. Blake, *Later History*, pp. 269, 281.

48. Henry Channing, *God Admonishing his People*, p. 25. The shift into deistic moralism is best detected in Channing's 1796 sermon delivered to the Masons in New London, the theme of which is fraternal benevolence. Acknowledged as the inculcator of charitable impulses, God is thereafter barely mentioned. *A Discourse Delivered in New London, at the Request of Union Lodge* (New London, 1796).

49. Blake, *Later History*, p. 274.

50. F.M. Caulkins, *History of New London* (New London, 1852), p. 588.

51. After leaving, he preached for a short time in the village of Canadaigua, in western New York. "I have a small congregation, who hear me with attention and treat me very affectionately." Joseph Felt, ed., *Memorials of William Smith Shaw* (Boston, 1852), p. 262.

53. Tappan, *Discourse Delivered in Chapel, September 16, 1794* (Cambridge, 1794), pp. 7, 10. Tappan, *Sermons on Important Subjects* (Boston, 1807), p. 267.

54. Tappan, *Discourse in Chapel*, p. 10.

55. For a provocative argument that Boston "excluded from its literature the telling of deeply personal truths; those truths which reveal the non-social self," and that its literature throughout the nineteenth century "bore the marks of the timid and flabby mind," see Martin Green, *The Problem of Boston* (New York: Norton, 1969), p. 192 and passim.

56. Josiah Quincy, *The History of Harvard University* (Boston 1860), II, 262; the quotation is from *The Panoplist*, I, 141.

57. Sidney Willard, *Memories of Youth and Manhood* (Boston, 1855), I, 263, 293.

58. Letter from William Ellery to Channing, 21 October 1794 (MHS).

59. WHC, *Memoir*, I, 54.

60. Letter from William Ellery to Channing, 10 July 1794 (MHS). The letter reveals a certain eagerness to see the boy move from Uncle Henry to Uncle Dana.

61. H. W. L. Dana, *The Dana Saga* (Cambridge: Cambridge Historical Society, 1941), p. 30.

62. Letter from William Ellery to Channing, 29 January 1797 (MHS).

63. Contemporaries report that his eloquence was universally admired. Willard, *Memories*, II, 17; W. W. Story, ed., *The Life and Letters of Joseph Story* (Boston, 1851), I, 53.

64. Library Charge List, 1795-1798, Harvard College Archives.

65. WHC, *Memoir*, I, 64.

66. Tappan, *Discourse in Chapel*, p. 14.

67. Elmer Sprague, "Francis Hutcheson," in *The Encyclopedia of Philosophy*, ed. Paul Edwards (New York: Macmillan, 1972), IV, 99. See Hutcheson, *Inquiry* (London, 1738), 4th ed., p. 122, for his argument that benevolence free from fear of future punishment and hope of future reward is the highest form of virtue.

68. WHC, *Memoir*, I, 78.

69. Hutcheson, *Inquiry*, pp. 99, 101.

70. Hutcheson, *Illustrations on the Moral Sense*, ed. Bernard Peach (Cambridge: Harvard University Press, 1971), p. 117.

71. WHC, *Memoir*, I, 64.

72. Ibid., I, 69, 70.

73. Felt, ed., *Memorials of Shaw*, p. 27.

74. WHC, *Memoir*, I, 72.

75. Ibid., I, 82-83.

76. Ibid., I, 106, 83, 97, 105.

77. Letter from William Ellery to Channing, 13 April 1799 (MHS).

78. WHC, *Memoir*, I, 104.

79. Ibid., I, 107.

80. Letters from William Ellery to Channing, 13 April 1799, 21 October 1794, and 13 April 1799 (MHS).

81. WHC, *Memoir*, I, 108.

82. Hutcheson, *Inquiry*, pp. 173, 212.

83. WHC, *Memoir*, I, 93.

84. Ibid., I, 111.

85. Robert Kiely, *The Romantic Novel in England* (Cambridge: Harvard University Press, 1972), p. 95.

86. WHC, *Memoir*, I, 85.

87. Ibid., I, 110.

88. Channing, *Works*, III, 306.

1. NATURE

1. Loren Eiseley, *Darwin's Century* (New York: Doubleday, 1961), p. 134.

2. *North American Review*, 60, no. 127 (April 1845), pp. 448, 439, 445-446.

3. William Hutchison, *The Transcendentalist Ministers* (Hamden, Conn: Archon Books, 1972), p. 82.

4. See Conrad Wright, *The Beginnings of Unitarianism in America* (Boston: Starr King Press, 1955), p. 151, for a somewhat different view.

5. See Perry Miller, "The Insecurity of Nature," in *Nature's Nation* (Cambridge: Harvard University Press, 1967), pp. 121-133.

6. Channing, *Works*, V, 177, 167, 168, 171; II, 280.

7. See Elizabeth McKinsey, *The Western Experiment: New England Transcendentalists in the Ohio Valley* (Cambridge: Harvard University Press, 1973), esp. p. 16.

8. Alan Heimert, *Religion and the American Mind from the Great Awakening to the Revolution* (Cambridge: Harvard University Press, 1966), pp. 156, 110, and passim.

9. Channing, *Works*, V, 171, 168.

10. Ibid., III, 379, 238; IV, 173-174.

11. See Channing, *The Perfect Life* (Boston, 1873), esp. pp. 176-183.

12. *A Treatise Concerning Religious Affections* (1746) (New Haven: Yale University Press, 1959), pp. 343, 398.

13. Channing, *Works*, V, 303.

14. Channing, *The Perfect Life*, p. 165; *Works*, III, 111-114.

15. W. H. Channing, "Jonathan Edwards and the Revivalists," *Christian Examiner*, 43 (4th ser., no. 8) (Nov. 1857), pp. 374-394.

16. Channing, *Works*, III, 382-383.

17. Ibid., III, 107, 383.

18. Ibid., II, 301, 311, 331.

19. Perry Miller, *The Transcendentalists* (Cambridge: Harvard University Press, 1950), p. 28.

20. See Joel Porte, "Religious Terror in Gothic Fiction," in *The Gothic Imagination: Essays in Dark Romanticism*, ed. G. R. Thompson (Pullman: Washington State University Press, 1974), pp. 42-64.

21. Channing, *Works*, V, 145-146.

22. Ibid., I, 74, 98, 130.

23. Edwards A. Park, "Memoir of Samuel Hopkins," pp. 90-91; and see the letter from Channing's grandfather, William Ellery, to Ezra Stiles on the sorry state of religion in Newport, in Abiel Holmes, *Life of Ezra Stiles* (Boston, 1795), pp. 223-224.

24. Channing, *Works*, II, 269.

25. *The Connecticut Wits*, ed. V. L. Parrington (New York: Crowell, 1969), p. 198.

26. Channing, *Works*, I, 95.

27. Orville Dewey, *Letters of an English Traveller* (Boston, 1828), p. 56.

28. Emerson, *Representative Men* (1850) (Boston, 1903), p. 241.

29. Channing, *Works*, II, 81.

30. Dewey, *English Traveller*, p. 57.

31. Emerson, *Representative Men*, p. 250. Carlyle, *Heroes, Hero Worship and The Heroic in History* (1841) (New York: A. L. Burt, n.d.) p. 282.

32. Channing, *Works*, I, 68.

33. Channing, *Works*, V, 174; IV, 124.

34. See Perry Miller, "Emersonian Genius and American Democracy," in *Nature's Nation*, pp. 163-174, and "Nature and the National Ego," in *Errand into the Wilderness* (Cambridge: Harvard University Press, 1956), pp. 204-216.

35. Channing, *Works*, VI, 155, 156; III, 146.

36. Kant, *Critique of Pure Reason*, trans. Norman Kemp Smith (New York: St. Martin's, 1965), p. 22.

37. Elizabeth Palmer Peabody, *Reminiscences of Dr. Channing* (Boston, 1877), p. 369. See also Siegfried Puknat, "Channing and German Thought," *Proceedings of the American Philosophical Society*, 101, no. 2 (April 1957), pp. 195-203.

38. Channing, *Works*, III, 115ff.

39. Ibid., III, 119, 238, 107.

40. Daniel Walker Howe, *The Unitarian Conscience: Harvard Moral Philosophy 1805-1861* (Cambridge: Harvard University Press, 1970), pp. 29-40.

41. René Wellek, *Confrontations* (Princeton: Princeton University Press, 1965), pp. 173, 178. See also John Weiss, *Life and Correspondence of Theodore Parker* (London, 1863), II, 454-455; and Andrews Norton, "Remarks on the Modern German School of Infidelity," in *Tracts Concerning Christianity* (Cambridge, 1852), esp. pp. 331-368.

42. For the concept's origins in seventeenth-century preparationism, see Perry Miller, "Preparation for Salvation in Seventeenth-Century New England," in *Nature's Nation*, pp. 50-77; and Norman Pettit, *The Heart Prepared* (New Haven: Yale University Press, 1966).

43. See Hutchison, *The Transcendentalist Ministers*, p. 90, and Howe, *The Unitarian Conscience*, pp. 79-80.

44. *Christian Examiner*, 24, no. 87 (3d ser., no. 18) (July 1838), p. 329.

45. Channing, *Works*, I, 50.

46. *North American Review*, 60, no. 127 (April 1845), p. 474.

47. See Douglas, *The Feminization of American Culture,* pp. 88-90.

48. Channing, *Works,* III, 397; II, 132; IV, 394; VI, 176; V, 33, 46; III, 310.

49. Ibid., III, 357.

50. Ibid., III, 301.

51. "The Interpretation of Channing," *The New England Quarterly,* 30, no. 1 (March 1957), 99-105.

52. *The Scarlet Letter* (1850) (Boston: Houghton Mifflin, 1961), p. 186.

53. *Boston Quarterly Review,* I, (October 1838), 505. *Christian Examiner,* 24, no. 87 (3d ser., no. 18) (July 1838), 329.

54. Samuel Johnson, *Preface to Shakespeare,* in *Rasselas, Poems, and Selected Prose,* ed. Bertrand H. Bronson (San Francisco: Rinehart, 1971), p. 267.

55. Channing, *Works,* III, 119, 249.

2. THE FLIGHT FROM HISTORY

1. WHC, *Memoir,* I, 34.

2. Channing, *Works,* IV, 353.

3. Hopkins, *Works,* II, 597-624. For another expression of Hopkins's uncompromising abolitionism, see Harriet Beecher Stowe, *The Minister's Wooing* (1859).

4. Channing, *Works,* IV, 394; V, 228.

5. Ibid., II, 204-205.

6. "Hawthorne and his Mosses" (1850), rpt. in *The Shock of Recognition,* ed. Edmund Wilson (New York: Doubleday, 1943), p. 192. *Twice-Told Tales* (1837) (New York: Washington Square Press, 1960), p. 96.

7. *Twice-Told Tales,* p. 94.

8. Channing, *Works,* II, 205; V, 68, 344-345.

9. Jefferson, *Notes on the State of Virginia* (New York: Norton, 1972), pp. 45ff. Georges L. L. Buffon, *Natural History* (1749-88) (London, 1797), VII, 38-39.

10. Robert M. Bird, *Nick of the Woods or the Jibbenainosay* (1837) (New Haven: College and University Press, 1967). Charles Brockden Brown, *Edgar Huntly* (1799) (New Haven: College and University Press, 1973), p. 171. W. H. Prescott, *The History of the Conquest of Mexico* (1843), ed. C. Harvey Gardiner (Chicago: University of Chicago Press, 1966), p. 264. Thoreau, *Walden* (1854) (New York: New American Library, 1960), p. 143. Poe, *The Narrative of A. Gordon*

Pym (1838), in *Selected Prose, Poetry, and Eureka*, ed. W. H. Auden (New York: Rinehart, 1950), p. 235.

11. *The Sketch Book* (New York: New American Library, 1961), pp. 133, 67, 43.

12. Channing, *Works*, II, 205.

13. Bancroft, *History of the United States* (Boston, 1844), I, 345ff. Parkman is quoted in David Levin, *History as Romantic Art* (New York: Harcourt, Brace, 1963), p. 35.

14. Channing, *Works*, III, 391.

15. Heimert, *Religion and the American Mind*, p. 126.

16. Letter to William Roscoe, 29 April 1828 (Liverpool Public Libraries).

17. Channing, *Works*, V, 84.

18. Ibid., IV, 394.

19. Ibid., IV, 163.

20. D. H. Fischer, *Growing Old in America* (New York: Oxford University Press, 1977), esp. pp. 66-112.

21. "The Escape from History," in *The Feminization of American Culture*, pp. 195, 189.

22. Edwards, *The Great Christian Doctrine of Original Sin Defended* (1758) (New Haven: Yale University Press, 1970), esp. pp. 398-401.

23. Channing, *Works*, V, 48, 199.

24. Ibid., V, 224-225.

25. Ibid., II, 233.

26. Ibid., II, 401-402.

27. Ibid., II, 209-210, 402, 270-271.

28. Ibid., IV, 161.

29. Ibid., II, 333.

30. Ibid., II, 258; VI, 317.

31. Henry May, *The Enlightenment in America* (New York: Oxford University Press, 1976), p. 6.

32. Charles M. Wiltse, *The New Nation* (New York: Hill and Wang, 1961), p. 106.

33. Channing, *Works*, V, 226, 163, 166; II, 360.

34. Ibid., IV, 381. See also III, 271.

35. Ibid., IV, 234.

36. Edwards, *The End for Which God Created the World*, in *Works*, ed. Edward Hickman (London, 1834), I, 101.

37. Edwards, *Miscellaneous Observations*, in *Works*, II, 698.

38. Karl Barth, *Protestant Thought from Rousseau to Ritschl* (New York: Simon and Schuster, 1969), p. 41.

39. WHC, *Memoir*, III, 118.

40. Edmund Wilson, *To the Finland Station* (New York: Double-day, 1953), pp. 131-132, 155.

41. Charles Chauncy, *Enthusiasm Described and Caution'd Against* (1742), in Alan Heimert and Perry Miller, eds., *The Great Awakening: Documents Illustrating the Crisis and Its Consequences* (New York: Bobbs-Merrill, 1967), p. 243.

42. Channing, *Works*, V, 49-50.

43. Perry Miller, *The Life of the Mind in America* (New York: Harcourt, Brace, 1967), pp. 128-129.

44. Channing, *Works*, VI, 249-250, 256, 267; V, 51, 104.

45. Ibid., V, 178.

46. Edwards, *A Narrative of Surprising Conversions* (1735) in Clarence Faust and Thomas Johnson, eds., *Edwards: Representative Selections* (New York: Hill and Wang, 1962), pp. 83-84.

47. See William Haller, *The Elect Nation* (New York: Harper, 1963).

48. Levin, *History as Romantic Art*, pp. 24-45.

49. Richard Hofstadter, *Anti-Intellectualism in American Life* (New York: Vintage, 1963), p. 83.

50. Channing, *Works*, II, 278.

51. Ibid., III, 60.

52. Dewey, *Letters of an English Traveller*, p. 81.

53. Channing, *Works*, III, 89, 129-130.

54. Ibid., V, 130.

55. Park, "Memoir of Hopkins," p. 83.

56. Channing, *Works*, III, 121.

57. Hutchison, *The Transcendentalist Ministers*, pp. 20, 87, 95.

58. Channing, *Works*, II, 275; III, 123.

59. Ibid., III, 108.

60. Ibid., III, 145.

61. Thomas Shepard, *Works*, ed. John Albro (Boston, 1853), III, 25-26.

62. Channing, *Works*, IV, 174.

63. Johnson, *Rasselas*, in Bronson, p. 668.

64. Channing, *Works*, IV, 394.

3. LANGUAGE AND THE NEUTRALITY OF SCRIPTURE

1. Peter Gay, *A Loss of Mastery: Puritan Historians in Colonial America* (Berkeley: University of California Press, 1966), pp. 88-117; Vincent Tomas, "The Modernity of Jonathan Edwards," *New England Quarterly*, 25 (1952), 60-84.

2. Edwards, *Works*, I, 116.

3. Miller, Introduction to Edwards, *Images or Shadows of Divine Things* (New Haven: Yale University Press, 1948), p. 19.

4. Samuel Miller, *Letters on Unitarianism* (Trenton, 1821), p. 44.

5. Channing, *Remarks on the Rev. Dr. Worcester's Letter to Mr. Channing* (Boston, 1815), p. 12.

6. See Earl Morse Wilbur, *A History of Unitarianism in Transylvania, England, and America* (Cambridge: Harvard University Press, 1952), pp. 420ff.

7. Jedediah Morse, *The True Reasons on Which the Election of a Hollis Professor of Divinity in Harvard College, Was Opposed at the Board of Overseers, Feb. 14, 1805* (Charlestown, 1805), p. 27.

8. *A Letter to the Rev. Samuel C. Thacher*, p. 17.

9. Ibid., p. 15.

10. *A Letter to the Rev. William E. Channing* (Boston, 1815), pp. 24, 33.

11. Miller, *Letters on Unitarianism*, p. 249.

12. See *The Monthly Anthology*, 2 (1805), p. 78.

13. Brownson, *The Convert* (1857), in Perry Miller, ed., *The Transcendentalists* (Cambridge: Harvard University Press, 1950), p. 46.

14. V. L. Parrington, *Main Currents in American Thought* (1927) (New York: Harcourt, Brace, 1954), II, 272.

15. *A Sermon Delivered at the Ordination of the Rev. John Codman* (Boston, 1808), p. 14.

16. William Perkins, *Works* (London, 1609), III, 438. Channing, *Codman Ordination Sermon*, p. 19.

17. *Codman Ordination Sermon*, p. 16.

18. Leonard Woods, *Works* (Andover, 1850), IV, 32. Moses Stuart, *Miscellanies* (Andover, 1846), p. 184.

19. *Codman Ordination Sermon*, p. 6.

20. *Nature* (1836), in Stephen E. Whicher, ed., *Emerson: An Organic Anthology*, (Boston: Houghton Mifflin, 1960), p. 52.

21. *Remarks on Worcester's Letter*, p. 30.

22. Beecher, *The Faith Once Delivered to the Saints* (Boston, 1823), p. 30.

23. See Sidney Mead, "Lyman Beecher and Connecticut Orthodoxy's Campaign Against the Unitarians, 1819-26," *Church History*, 9 (1940), 218-234; and Howe, *The Unitarian Conscience*, pp. 219-220.

24. *Remarks on Worcester's Letter*, pp. 23-24.

25. Philip Gura, *The Philosophy of Language: The Dialogue in Transcendentalist Circles* (Ph.D. diss., Harvard University, 1977), p. 39.

37. Channing, *Works*, V, 310, 303, 298.

38. Ibid., V, 299.

39. Douglas Stange, *Patterns of Anti-Slavery among American Unitarians* (Cranbury, New Jersey: Associated University Presses, 1977), p. 56.

40. Channing, *Works*, V, 97.

41. Hopkins, *Works*, II, 553-54.

42. *Regeneration through Violence* (Middletown, Conn.: Wesleyan University Press, 1973).

43. See G. H. Barnes, *The Anti-Slavery Impulse*, p. 44.

44. *Love and Death in the American Novel* (London: Paladin, 1970), p. 248.

45. Channing, *Works*, III, 314.

46. See *The Life and Letters of John Greenleaf Whittier*, ed. S. T. Pickard (Boston, 1895), I, 136-138; and Albert Mordell, *Quaker Militant: John Greenleaf Whittier* (Boston: Houghton Mifflin, 1933), p. 73.

47. *The Writings of John Greenleaf Whittier* (Boston, 1888-89), III, 130.

48. Ezra Stiles Gannett, *Discourse Preached in the Federal Street Meetinghouse, Sunday June 11, 1854* (Boston, 1854), pp. 5, 7.

49. *Walden and Other Writings* (New York: Modern Library, 1950), p. 704.

50. Henry James, *The Bostonians* (1886) (Baltimore: Penguin, 1975), pp. 328, 97, 26, 87, 92, 338-339.

51. Channing, *Works*, VI, 103.

52. Ibid., IV, 290-292.

53. *The Problem of Slavery in Western Culture* (Ithaca: Cornell University Press, 1966), pp. 91-94.

54. Channing, *Works*, II, 58; III, 23.

55. Barnes, *the Anti-Slavery Impulse*, p. 162.

56. Finney, *Lectures to Professing Christians* (New York, 1837), p. 9.

57. Channing, *Works*, VI, 244, 254.

58. Ibid., VI, 255, 277.

59. *Pierre, or the Ambiguities* (New York: New American Library, 1964), p. 96.

60. Channing, *Works*, VI, 267.

61. *The American Whigs*, ed. Daniel Walker Howe (New York: Wiley, 1973), pp. 30-31.

62. See George Tucker, "Examination of the Political Objections to a National Bank" (1839), in *The American Whigs*, pp. 44-50.

63. Channing, *Works*, IV, 60-65; III, 75, 170-187.

64. Ibid., II, 197.

65. Ibid., VI, 293, 322.

66. John Quincy Adams, *Memoirs*, X, 40.

67. Channing, *Works*, IV, 158.

68. Ibid., VI, 72.

69. See George Fredrickson, *The Inner Civil War*, esp. pp. 151-180.

70. Brown, *Life against Death* (1959) (Middletown: Wesleyan University Press, 1970), p. 223.

71. *Religion and the American Mind*, pp. 330-331, 355, 481-489.

72. Channing, *Works*, V, 243.

73. Mill, *Autobiography* (1873) (London: Oxford University Press, 1969), p. 123.

74. Joel Porte, *Emerson and Thoreau: Transcendentalists in Conflict* (Middletown: Wesleyan University Press, 1966), p. 192.

75. *The Education of Henry Adams* (1907) (Boston: Houghton Mifflin, 1961), p. 380.

5. CHANNING AND ROMANTICISM

1. Alfred Cobban, *Edmund Burke and the Revolt against the Eighteenth Century* (London, 1929), p. 16, quoted in Basil Willey, *The Seventeenth-Century Background* (New York: Anchor, 1963), p. 264.

2. Peter Gay, *The Enlightenment: An Interpretation: The Rise of Modern Paganism* (New York: Norton, 1977), p. 419.

3. Sereno Dwight, *The Life of President Edwards* (New York, 1830), p. 30.

4. Locke, *Essay concerning Human Understanding*, II, xx, 4-14.

5. Channing, *The Perfect Life*, p. 142.

6. Channing, *Works*, IV, 87.

7. Locke, *Essay*, II, i, 19.

8. WHC, *Memoir*, I, 249.

9. Letter to Susan Higginson Channing, 24 August 1811 (Pierpont Morgan Library).

10. Channing, *Works*, III, 44.

11. *A Protest against the War* (Newburyport, 1812), p. 12. For another example, see Noah Worcester, *Abraham and Lot* (Concord, 1812), which puts the matter somewhat more subtly: "It is my opinion, that more pains would be taken to avoid the evils of war, if *officers* of government were compelled to take the place of *soldiers* in the day of battle" (p. 11).

12. Channing, *A Sermon Preached in Boston, September 18, 1814* (Boston, 1814), p. 11.

13. Letter to Susan Higginson Channing, 21 July 1812 (Pierpont Morgan Library).

14. Channing, *Works*, V, 311.

15. WHC, *Memoir*, II, 175.

16. Ibid., II, 193.

17. Channing, *Works*, VI, 380.

18. See Howe, *The Unitarian Conscience*, esp. pp. 36-38; and Merle Curti, "The Great Mr. Locke: America's Philosopher 1783-1861," *Huntington Library Bulletin*, 11 (April 1937), 107-151.

19. Locke, *Essay*, II, xi, 12-13.

20. *Rousseau and Romanticism* (1919) (New York: Meridian, 1955), pp. 120-121.

21. WHC, *Memoir*, I, 66.

22. Leibniz, Preface to *New Essays on the Human Understanding*, in *Philosophical Writings*, ed. G. H. R. Parkinson (London: Dent, 1973), p. 152.

23. *Tristram Shandy*, ed. Douglas Grant (Cambridge: Harvard University Press, 1970), pp. 33, 388.

24. Channing, *Works*, V, 33; II, 223.

25. David Perkins, *The Quest for Permanence* (Cambridge: Harvard University Press, 1959), p. 13.

26. "Wordsworth: A Minority Report," in *British Romantic Poets: Recent Revaluations*, ed. S. K. Kumar (New York: New York University Press, 1966), p. 40. See also Perkins, *The Quest for Permanence*, p. 25.

27. *The Idea of History* (New York: Oxford University Press, 1956), p. 82.

28. *A Preface to Paradise Lost* (New York: Oxford University Press, 1961), pp. 62-65.

29. Channing, *Works*, III, 142.

30. *Reason and Revolution* (Boston: Beacon Press, 1960), pp. 18-19.

31. *Experience* (1843), and *Self-Reliance* (1841) in Whicher, pp. 270, 149.

32. Channing, *Works*, IV, 151-152.

33. Aleksandr Solzhenitsyn, *Commencement Address* (Cambridge: Harvard University Gazette, 8 June 1978), p. 19.

34. Channing, *Works*, I, 36, 7, 8. Emerson, *Self-Reliance*, in Whicher, p. 147.

35. Channing, *Works*, I, 94, 108, 72, 114.

36. Ibid., I, 79-80.

37. "Preliminary Essay," in Coleridge, *Aids to Reflection* (Burlington, Vt., 1840), pp. 34, 48.

38. Quoted in Robert Leet Patterson, *The Philosophy of William Ellery Channing* (New York: Bookman, 1952), p. 289.

39. *The Genteel Tradition* (1911) (Cambridge: Harvard University Press, 1967), p. 43.

40 Friedrich Schiller, *On the Aesthetic Education of Man* (1793), trans. Reginald Snell (New York: Frederick Ungar, 1965), p. 87.

41. Channing, *Works,* I, 8, 13.

42. Ibid., VI, 286.

43. WHC, *Memoir,* II, 446.

44. Heimert, *Religion and the American Mind,* p. 551.

45. Channing, *Works,* VI, 66-67; I, 110, xx; V, 130.

Index

Simpson, ed., *The Federalist Literary Mind* (Baton Rouge: Louisiana State University Press, 1962), p. 98.

16. John Quincy Adams, *Memoirs* (12 vols., Philadelphia, 1876), IX, 265.

17. Simpson, *The Federalist Literary Mind*, p. 100.

18. Channing, *Works*, I, 53.

19. Edward Strutt Abdy, *Journal of a Residence and Tour in the United States* (London, 1835), III, 222, 233. *Letters of Lydia Marie Child* (Boston, 1883), pp. 48, 144.

20. *Letters of James G. Birney*, ed. Dwight L. Dumond (New York: Appleton-Century, 1938), I, 372-373.

21. Garrison, *Thoughts* (Boston, 1832), p. 9.

22. David Donald, *Lincoln Reconsidered* (New York: Vintage, 1961), p. 33. A defense of radical abolitionism has been eloquently argued by Aileen Kraditor, *Means and Ends in American Abolitionism* (New York: Pantheon, 1969).

23. See, for example, Gilbert H. Barnes, *The Anti-Slavery Impulse* (1933) (New York: Harcourt, Brace, 1964); and Dwight L. Dumond, *Anti-Slavery Origins of the Civil War* (1939) (Ann Arbor: University of Michigan Press, 1959).

24. Channing, *Works*, II, 126.

25. Ibid., II, 130.

26. *A Treatise Concerning Religious Affections*, pp. 393-394.

27. Channing, *Works*, II, 7. Channing was aware of a spreading conviction that slavery was less profitable than free labor; II, 82.

28. Samuel J. May, *Some Recollections of our Anti-Slavery Conflict* (Boston, 1869), pp. 174-175.

29. Channing, *Works*, V, 27; II, 107, 108.

30. Ibid., V, 17.

31. For an argument that places abolition in the larger context of American anti-institutionalism, see Stanley Elkins, *Slavery*, 2nd ed. (Chicago: University of Chicago Press, 1968).

32. Channing, *Works*, V, 234.

33. Child, *Letters*, p. 46.

34. For a discussion of romantic theodicy, see M. H. Abrams, *Natural Supernaturalism* (New York: Norton, 1971), pp. 187-195.

35. Schleiermacher, *On Religion: Speeches to Its Cultured Despisers*, trans. John Oman (New York: Harper, 1958), p. 68. For the sources of this view, and for the history of theodicy generally, see John Hick, *Evil and the God of Love*, rev. ed. (New York: Harper, 1978).

36. Channing, *Works*, V, 243; I, 23. Bancroft, *History of the United States* (Boston, 1843), III, 98.

78. Hazard, *Language* (Boston, 1836), p. 90.

79. See Elizabeth Peabody, *Reminiscences of Dr. Channing* (Boston, 1880), p. 372; and Hutchison, *The Transcendentalist Ministers*, p. 90. Hazard, *Language*, p. 76.

80. *Remarks on Worcester's Second Letter*, p. 18.

81. *Letter from a Gentleman in Boston to a Unitarian Clergyman* (Boston, 1828), p. 16.

82. WHC, *Memoir*, II, 445.

83. Thomas Shepard, *Works* (Boston, 1853), III. 17.

84. Stuart, *Miscellanies*, p. 180.

85. Samuel Miller, *Letters on Unitarianism*, p. 197.

86. Channing, *Works*, III, 134-135.

87. See Ernest Lee Tuveson, *Redeemer Nation* (Chicago: University of Chicago Press, 1968), p. 13.

88. Channing, *Works*, III, 224, 221-222.

89. M. H. Abrams, *Natural Supernaturalism*, chap. 1, esp. pp. 56ff.

90. "The Background of the Unitarian Opposition to Transcendentalism," *Modern Philology*, 35 (1938), 297-324.

91. Henry Steele Commager, ed., *Theodore Parker: An Anthology* (Boston: Beacon Press, 1960), pp. 75-76.

4. SLAVERY AND THE PROBLEM OF EVIL

1. Channing, *Works*, V, 29-30.

2. *The Enlightenment in America* (New York: Oxford University Press, 1976).

3. *The Connecticut Wits*, ed. V. L. Parrington (New York: Apollo, 1969), pp. 256, 260.

4. Joseph Bellamy, *Works* (Boston, 1850), I, 585, 588, 578, 586, 596.

5. Ibid., II, 1-17; I, 583-584, 75-76.

6. Ibid., II, 7; Samuel Hopkins, *Works* (Boston, 1852), III, 727.

7. WHC, *Memoir*, I, 139.

8. Hopkins, *Works*, III, 731.

9. Bellamy, *Works*, I, 457.

10. Hopkins, *Works*, II, 325-326, 263.

11. Channing, *Works*, I, 131-132.

12. Ibid., I, 25, 36.

13. Irving, *The Sketch Book* (1820) (New York: New American Library, 1961), p. 26.

14. "The Dangers and Duties of Men of Letters" (1809), in Lewis P.

52. For the debate over Channing's proximity to the Transcendentalists, see Conrad Wright, "The Rediscovery of Channing," in *The Liberal Christians* (Boston: Beacon Press, 1970), pp. 22-40; David P. Edgell, *William Ellery Channing: An Intellectual Portrait* (Boston: Beacon Press, 1955), esp. pp. 113-149; Arthur I. Ladu, "Channing and Transcendentalism," *American Literature*, 11 (1939), 129-137.

53. *The Divinity School Address* (1838), in Whicher, p. 105.

54. Channing, *Works*, V, 290-291.

55. Bate, *From Classic to Romantic* (1946) (New York: Harper, 1961), p. 12.

56. Channing, *Works*, II, 14; V, 291.

57. Ibid., V, 313.

58. Ibid., V, 190.

59. John Cotton, *A Brief Exposition of the Whole Book of Canticles* (1642), and Thomas Hooker, *Preface* to *A Survey of the Summe of Church-Discipline* (1648), quoted in Perry Miller and Thomas Johnson, *The Puritans* (New York: Harper, 1963), II, 666, 673.

60. Channing, *Works*, V, 305, 288; II, 317; III, 281.

61. Ibid., III, 254. See also Howe, *The Unitarian Conscience*, p. 173.

62. Douglas, *The Feminization of American Culture*, p. 85.

63. Miller, *The Life of the Mind in America*, p. 7. Channing, *Works*, III, 147.

64. *In Defense of Reason* (Chicago: The Swallow Press, n.d.) p. 383.

65. Channing, *Works*, I, 110-111, 37.

66. WHC, *Memoir*, I, 274.

67. Channing, *Works*, V, 305.

68. *The Mirror and the Lamp* (New York: Oxford University Press, 1953), p. 14.

69. Channing, *Works*, I, xxi.

70. Ibid., V, 288.

71. Douglas, *The Feminization of American Culture*, p. 42.

72. Henry Ware, Jr., *Hints on Extemporaneous Preaching* (Boston, 1824), pp. 12-13.

73. Channing, *Works*, II, 267.

74. David Hackett Fischer, *The Revolution of American Conservatism* (New York: Harper, 1965), pp. 12, 153-154.

75. Channing, *Works*, I, 21-22.

76. Richard Altick, *The English Common Reader* (Chicago: University of Chicago Press, 1957), p. 121.

77. Emerson, *The Poet* (1843), in Whicher, p. 236.

26. See Gura, *Philosophy of Language*, esp. pp. 42-45; Lawrence Buell, *Literary Transcendentalism* (Ithaca: Cornell University Press, 1973), p. 33; and Jerry Wayne Brown, *The Rise of Biblical Criticism in America: 1800-1870* (Middletown: Wesleyan University Press, 1969), esp. pp. 75-93.

27. Channing, *Remarks on the Rev. Dr. Worcester's Second Letter to Mr. Channing* (Boston, 1815), p. 17.

28. See Conrad Wright, *The Beginnings of Unitarianism in America* (Boston: Starr King Press, 1955), p. 200; and, for a discussion of the same issue as it confronted a rational Puritan, Jesper Rosenmeier, "New England's Perfection: The Image of Adam and the Image of Christ in the Antinomian Crisis," *William and Mary Quarterly*, 17 (1970), 435-459.

29. *Remarks on Worcester's Second Letter*, pp. 22, 17. Channing, *Works*, III, 176.

30. *Remarks on Worcester's Second Letter*, p. 46.

31. *A Sermon Preached in Boston, August 20, 1812, The Day of Humiliation and Prayer* (Boston, 1812), p. 18.

32. Channing, *Works*, II, 102-103.

33. Stuart, *Miscellanies*, pp. 182, 79.

34. See his *Conscience and the Constitution* (Boston, 1850).

35. Stuart, *Miscellanies*, p. 25.

36. Ibid., pp. 13-14.

37. Channing, *Works*, III, 66.

38. Woods, *Works*, IV, 20-21, 13-14.

39. Miller, *Letters on Unitarianism*, p. 201.

40. Woods, *Works*, IV, 127. Ware, *Letters to Trinitarians and Calvinists* (Boston, 1820), p. 14.

41. Miller, *Letters on Unitarianism*, p. 285.

42. Parrington, *Main Currents*, II, 322.

43. *Letter to Thacher*, p. 17,

44. *Remarks on Worcester's Second Letter*, p. 43.

45. *Remarks on Worcester's Letter*, "Notes," p. 2.

46. *The Faith Once Delivered to the Saints*, p. 13.

47. Henry Ware, Jr., *The Faith Once Delivered to the Saints* (Boston, 1827), p. 9. Channing, *Remarks on Worcester's Second Letter*, p. 22.

48. *Moby Dick* (1851) (Indianapolis and New York: Bobbs-Merrill, 1964), p. 555.

49. *Remarks on Worcester's Second Letter*, p. 39.

50. Ibid., p. 38.

51. Channing, *Works*, III, 167; see also Hutchison, *The Transcendentalist Ministers*, p. 5.